W0007879

LOCOMOTIVES

LOCOMOTIVES

By Christopher Chant; edited by John Moore

Grange BOOKS

Published in 2002 by
Grange Books
An imprint of Grange Books Plc
The Grange
Kingsnorth Industrial Estate
Hoo, nr Rochester
Kent ME3 9ND
www.grangebooks.co.uk

ISBN 1 84013 329 5

Printed in Hong Kong

PAGE 2: Replicas of Stephenson's Rocket *and Cooper's* Tom Thumb.

TITLE PAGE: Puffing Billy, *William Hedley's locomotive patented in 1813. It began work in that year and continued in use until 1872. From a set of cigarette cards published in 1901.*

RIGHT: Replica Planet crossing Swithland viaduct on the Great Central Railway, England.

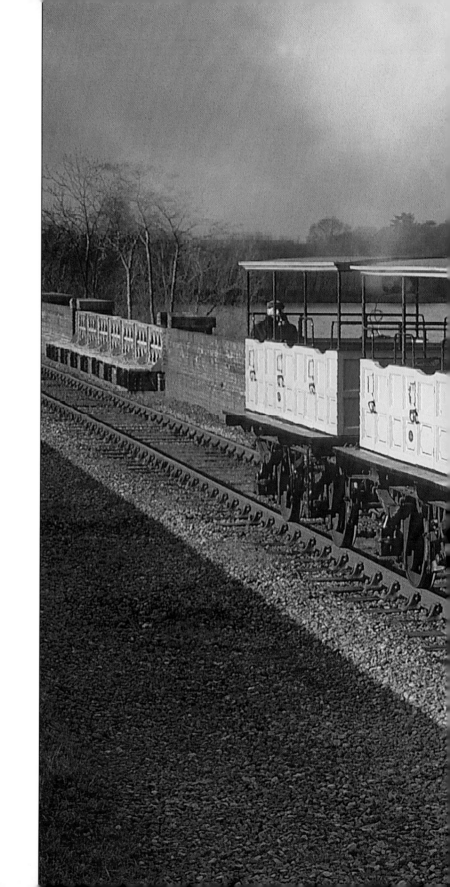

LOCOMOTIVES

The working of a steam locomotive is based on the use of the physical principle that water heated to a temperature above boiling point tries to become steam, in the process expanding in volume about 1,000 times. Kept inside the boiler, the steam is confined in volume and its pressure therefore increases, but once moved to a piston-fitted cylinder it drives the piston down the cylinder. This movement of the piston is transferred to the wheels by a system of connecting rods, the pressure of the steam thus being translated into the rotation of the wheels.

In essence, therefore, the steam locomotive comprises the two separate but indispensable elements of the boiler and the engine. The former is a closed unit that, in the majority of steam locomotives, also comprises a rear-located firebox and tubes to lead the fire's hot gases through the boiler proper (braced internally by large numbers of stays to resist the steam pressure) to a front-mounted smokebox. A valve, known as the regulator (in fact the throttle), controls the movement of steam along the steam pipe to the engine from which, after the majority of its useful energy has been extracted, it is removed by means of the blast-pipe into the smokebox and thence up the chimney. The

steam emerging from the blast-pipe creates a partial vacuum in the smokebox and thus helps significantly in 'drawing' the fire in the firebox in a fashion directly proportional to the amount of steam being used in a neat arrangement which ensures that the more steam is used (and therefore needed), the more steam is made.

The fires of most steam locomotives are of the coal-burning type with the fire burning on a grate of iron firebars through which the ashes fall into an ashpan. Other elements of the boiler include a method for filling the boiler with water (and then of replacing the water that has been turned to steam and used before being exhausted) from a water tank that is fitted on the locomotive itself or on a towed tender: a steam locomotive with onboard tank(s) is a tank locomotive, while that with a towed tender is a tender locomotive.

The structural core of the engine proper is a number of frames fabricated from iron (later steel) plates or bars, or alternatively produced as a single casting. In this unit are the slots for the axle-boxes carrying the wheel sets, each comprising a pair of wheels on a single axle: the axle-boxes are attached to the frames by springs to provide shock absorption. Each containing a single piston,

OPPOSITE: A commemorative medal of Scottish engineer and inventor James Watt, the inventor of the first condensing steam engine.

BELOW: An interesting painting illustrating progress in the 19th century, showing telegraph, printing press, steam ship and railway.

BOTTOM LEFT: Guyot's Steam Carriage of 1769, an example of a steam locomotive.

BOTTOM RIGHT: Timothy Hackworth's Royal George locomotive of 1826.

BELOW: Trevithick's Coalbrookdale locomotive, 1803. Museum drawing based on an original contemporary sketch. A single horizontal cylinder, 4.75 x 36in (121 x 914mm), enclosed in a cast-iron return-flue boiler and provided with a flywheel, drove the wheels on one side only through spur gears. Steam was distributed through valve plugs worked by tappets. The cylinder was placed at the same end of the boiler as the furnace door and boiler pressure was around 50lb/sq in (3.5kg/cm^2). There were cast-iron plate rails, and axles were mounted directly on the boiler, without a separate frame. There were no flanges on the wheels.

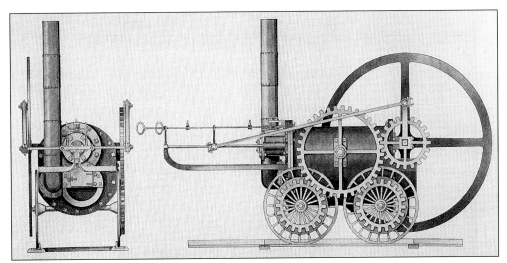

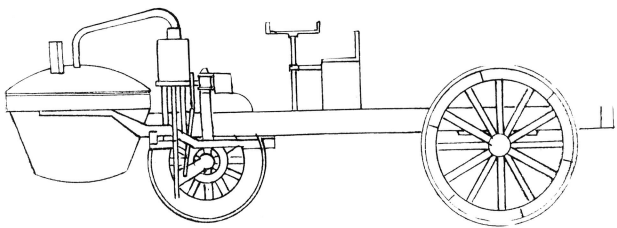

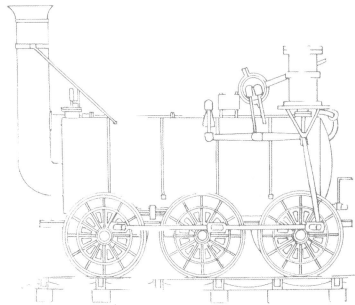

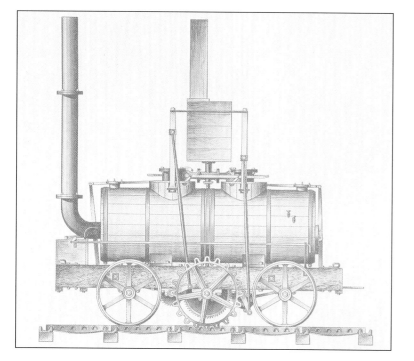

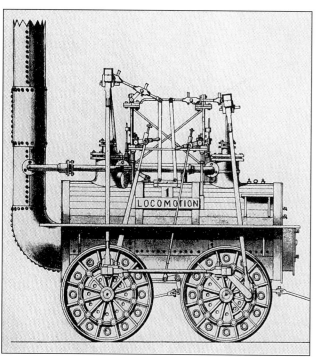

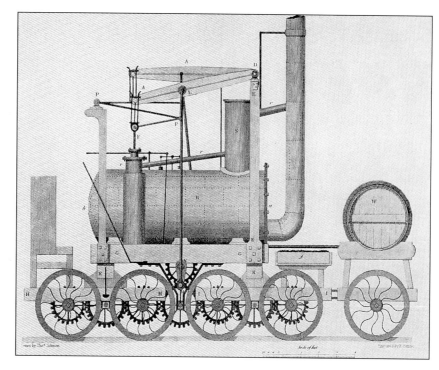

ABOVE LEFT: *Blenkinsop's rack locomotive, 1812.*

ABOVE: *Braithwaite and Erricsson's 0-2-2* Novelty *well-tank locomotive of 1829.*

FAR LEFT: *Stephenson's 0-4-0* Locomotion *of 1825 for the Stockton & Darlington Railway.*

LEFT: *Hedley's 0-8-0 locomotive for Wylam, 1813–14.*

OPPOSITE: *Trevithick's 0-4-0 Newcastle locomotive of 1805, probably the first railway locomotive with flanged wheels. The rails would have been made from wood and too weak, so the track was later made of iron.*

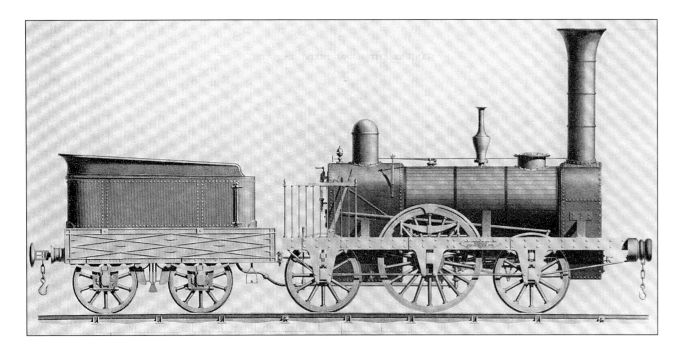

the cylinders are attached to the frames, and the driving force of the pistons as each is driven by the admission of steam to its cylinder (alternately at each end) is communicated to the wheels by a rod-and-guide system, this comprising a cross head and one or more guide bars. A circular-section piston rod connects the piston to the cross head by means of a steam-tight gland in the end of the cylinder, and a connecting-rod attaches the cross head to the driving wheels, with drive to other pairs of wheels possible by the addition of coupling rods.

A valve or valves are used to duct the steam into or out of the end of the cylinder when and (according to the direction and speed of movement) where it is required. These valves are linked with the wheels by means of valve gear. There have been

many types of valves and associated valve gears, but all work on the concept that admission of steam into one end of a piston-fitted cylinder will result in movement of the piston with a force based on the steam's pressure and the piston head's area.

The development of the boiler and steam engine in terms of efficiency and power is, inevitably, the driving force behind the design and manufacture of the great steam locomotives in the 'golden age' of steam, the period between the success of the *Rocket* in the Rainhill Trials of October 1829 and the outbreak of World War II (1939–45).

Although it was the Stephenson *Rocket* that secured victory over four other contenders (*Novelty*, *Sans Pareil*, *Cycloped* and *Perseverance*) in the Rainhill Trials to

select the locomotive for the passenger service soon to be inaugurated by the Liverpool & Manchester Railway, the steam locomotive actually used for this first inter-city service on 15 September 1830 was the *Northumbrian*. This was superior in several important respects to the *Rocket*, having a smokebox for the accumulation of ashes drawn through the boiler tubes and the integration of the boiler with the water jacket round the firebox, in effect creating for the first time the locomotive type of boiler that was to become wholly standard. Another improvement was the location of the cylinders with their axes in an almost horizontal position rather than the ungainly angle of some 35° used in the *Rocket* and causing the locomotive to rock. In addition, the cylinders of the

Northumbrian were installed in a readily accessible position outside the wheels. The *Northumbrian* massed 16,465lb (7469kg) without its tender, a weight nearly twice that of the *Rocket*, and the locomotive's potential for causing damage was reflected in the installation of a front buffer beam carrying horsehair-filled leather buffers. Finally, a proper tender rather than merely a barrel on wheels was used.

The features that made the *Rocket* a success at the Rainhill Trials were continued in the *Northumbrian*, albeit in forms that were stronger and larger. The multi-tube type of boiler (one with many tubes rather than one substantial pipe to conduct the hot gases through the water in the boiler) was again used as it was now clear that the greater area of multiple small tubes provided superior heating capability,

OPPOSITE LEFT: Stephenson's 2-2-2 standard passenger engine. Cylinders were 12 x 18in (305 x 457mm), the boiler was under pressure to the extent of 50lb/sq in (3.5kg/cm²), and the wheelbase was 9ft 2in (2.75m). It had four eccentric valve gears.

RIGHT: Timothy Hackworth's locomotive Sans Pareil. *From Luke Herbert's* Engineer's and Mechanic's Encyclopedia, *London, 1836.*

and so too was the other highly significant feature of the *Rocket*, namely the blast-pipe to ensure the exhaust of the spent steam up the smokestack to create a partial vacuum at the forward end of the whole boiler arrangement to create greater draw in the firebox at the rear of the boiler. The *Northumbrian* possessed just two cylinders outside the frames and directly connected to the driving wheels in the pattern that rapidly became and remained the norm for

all but articulated steam locomotives.

The positive features of the *Northumbrian* should not be construed as meaning that this pioneering steam locomotive lacked poorer features. The two large driving wheels were located toward the front, so the positioning of the heavy firebox and the heavy cylinders at the rear, over the two small carrying wheels, where their weight was offset only by the relatively light smokebox forward

of the driving wheels, meant that tractive effort was reduced, a process exacerbated by the action of the drawbar, which tended to lift the front end of the locomotive.

Another problem resulted from the combination of outside cylinders and a short wheelbase, which caused the locomotive to sway directionally until it was revised with a longer wheelbase and the cylinders shifted to the front.

Another failing in the *Northumbrian*

THIS PAGE: A replica of the Northumbrian *at the Derby works circa 1930, built by Stephenson for the Liverpool & Manchester Railway in 1830. After the Rainhill Trials in 1829, locomotive development was very rapid.*

was the lack of any effective means to reverse the drive while the locomotive was in motion, and this feature proved disastrous when William Huskisson, MP, stepped in front of the *Rocket* and was severely injured as the driver had no means of stopping quickly. Huskisson was rushed to medical aid by the *Northumbrian*, but died of his injuries.

The *Northumbrian* is usually listed as a member of the 'Rocket' class, of which seven had been delivered to the Liverpool & Manchester Railway in 1829 and 1830. Those immediately following the *Rocket* were the *Meteor*, the *Comet*, the *Dart* and the *Arrow* with their cylinders almost horizontal, and the *Rocket* was rapidly altered to the same condition. The *Phoenix* and the *North Star* each possessed a smokebox, while the *Majestic*, which followed the *Northumbrian*, possessed all the new features.

The specification for the *Northumbrian* included a 0-2-2 layout, a tractive effort of 1,580lb (717kg), two 11 x 16-in (280 x 406-mm) cylinders, driving wheels with a diameter of 4ft 4in (1.321m), a steam pressure of about 50lb/sq in (3.5kg/cm^2), about 2,200lb (998kg) of coke fuel, about 480 U.S. gal (400 Imp gal; 1818 litres) of water, total weight of 25,500lb (11567kg), and overall length of 24ft 0in (7.315m).

The successor class introduced on the Liverpool & Manchester Railway from October 1830 was the 'Planet' class of 2-2-0 steam locomotives. The new type reflected the rapidly developing design concepts of the two Stephensons, and as such had two

forward-mounted horizontal cylinders, which enhanced the locomotive's weight distribution, as well as the driving wheels at the rear under the firebox, whose weight now improved the locomotive's adherence to the rails. Another significant improvement, introduced to eliminate the tendency of earlier locomotives to sway as the drive power switched from one wheel to the other, was the relocation of the cylinders inside the wheels to drive the axle by means of a double-crank.

The Planet class was relatively successful and many of these engines, some of them with four coupled wheels, were manufactured by the Stephensons and also by others including, perhaps most importantly, Matthias Baldwin of Philadelphia in the U.S.A. who in 1832 produced the *Old Ironsides*. This was the first full-size steam locomotive from a company that became the world's most prolific manufacturer of such engines, totalling some 60,000 over a period of 130 years.

In historical terms it was the Planet class that may rightly be seen as the steam locomotive that proved beyond doubt that the age of mechanical transport was safe and not just feasible but commercially viable. It was the success of the Planet class that in reality lifted the Stephensons into the 'millionaire' bracket and led to their acceptance as the true originators of rail transport.

The other data for the Planet class included a tractive effort of about 1,450lb (658kg), two 11.5 x 16-in (292 x 406-mm)

OPPOSITE ABOVE: Robert Stephenson's locomotive Planet, *1830.*

BELOW: Stephenson's Rocket *0-2-2 locomotive for the Liverpool & Manchester Railway, 1829. A museum drawing based on remains and contemporary illustrations and descriptions.*

THIS PAGE
ABOVE: The Best Friend of Charleston, *built in 1830 by the West Point Foundry for use on the South Carolina Canal & Railroad Company.*

BELOW: A selection of locomotives with, from left to right, the Batavia *built by the Baldwin Locomotive Works for Tonawanda Railroad, the locomotive* America, *Baldwin's* Old Ironsides, *built for the Philadelphia, Germantown & Norristown Railroad, 1832, and one of the first 4-2-0 locomotives built by Baldwin for the Utica & Schenectady Railroad, 1837.*

cylinders, driving wheels with a diameter of 5ft 2in (1.575m), steam pressure of about 50lb/sq in (3.5kg/cm^2), about 2,200lb (998kg) of coke fuel, about 480 U.S. gal (400 Imp gal; 1818 litres) of water, total weight of 29,500lb (13381kg) and overall length of 24ft 4in (7.42m).

It was on 15 January 1831 that the first full-size steam locomotive manufactured in the U.S.A. entered service. This was the *Best Friend of Charleston*, an odd 0-4-0 locomotive operating on America's first commercial steam railroad, the South Carolina Canal & Railroad. Made by the West Point Foundry in New York late in 1830 to the design of E. L. Miller, the *Best Friend of Charleston* had a vertical boiler, a well tank manufactured integral with the locomotive, four coupled wheels and two modestly inclined cylinders. None of the locomotive's features except the coupled wheels became standard, but the *Best Friend of Charleston* was nonetheless successful at the technical level and could pull five carriages, carrying 50 or more passengers, at 20mph (32km/h). The explosion of the locomotive's boiler in 1831, after the

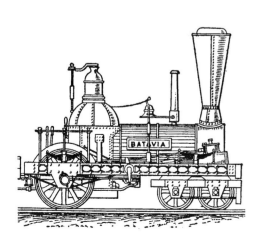

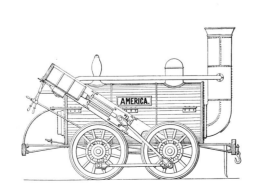

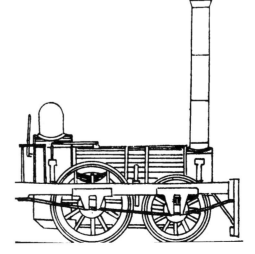

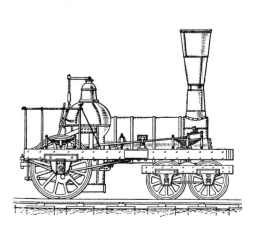

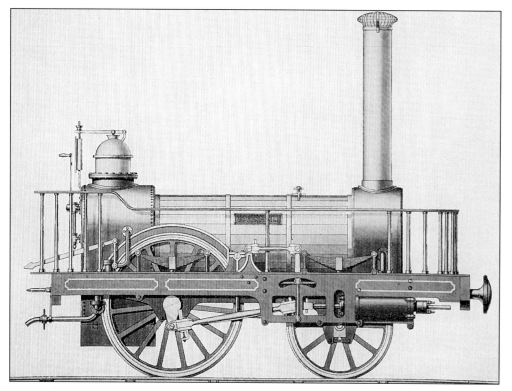

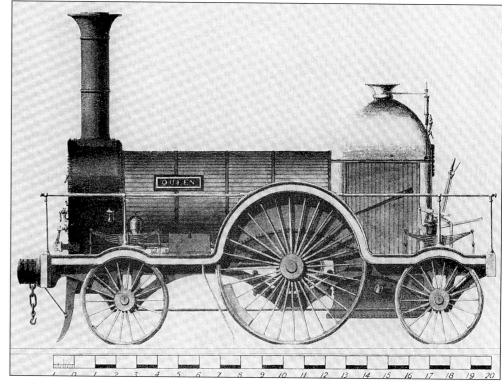

ABOVE LEFT: *Forrester's 2-2-0* Vauxhall *locomotive of the Dublin & Kingstown Railway, 1834. It had horizontal outside cylinders of 11 x 18in (279 x 457mm), with vibrating pillar parallel motion and was said to have had four eccentric gab valve gear.*

LEFT: *The 4-2-0 locomotive* Experiment *built by John B. Jervis at the West Point Foundry, U.S.A. in 1832.*

ABOVE: *Gooch's 2-2-2 Prince-class* Queen *locomotive of the Great Western Railway of 1847, from a watercolour by E.T. Lane dated 3 July 1849. It had a broad-gauge engine with inside sandwich frame and cylinders of 18 x 24in (457 x 610mm). Boiler pressure was around 100lb/sq in (7kg/cm²) and the heating surface was 1081sq ft (100m²). Weight was around 26.2 tons and the locomotive had a wheelbase of 14ft 10in (4.5m).*

OPPOSITE: *Stephenson's 0-2-2 locomotive* Northumbrian, *Liverpool & Manchester Railway, 1830. From an engraving by I. Shaw, 1831. It was generally similar to the* Rocket, *but the cylinders were nearly horizontal and the boiler had an internal firebox and smokebox. The main frames were formed of vertical plates to which the axle-box horns were bolted.*

was later transformed into a 4-4-0 layout, and among its details were a tractive effort of about 1,023lb (464kg), two 9.5 x 16-in (241 x 406-mm) cylinders, driving wheels with a diameter of 5ft 0in (1.52m), boiler pressure of about 50lb/sq in (3.5kg/cm²), weight of 14,999lb (6804kg) without tender, and length of 16ft 5.5in (5.017m) without tender.

The 'Vauxhall'-class locomotive, designed and built for the Dublin & Kingstown Railway of Ireland in 1834 by George Forrester, introduced two important features to the concept of the steam locomotive. The first of these was the installation of the cylinders outside the driving wheels in a horizontal position at the front of the locomotive in a position in which they were effective and also readily accessible; here the pistons and connecting rods powered the driving wheels by means of separate cranks on the outside of the wheels. Of greater importance was the provision for the first time of an effective mechanism to reverse the drive, although the locomotive had first to be halted before the reverse system could be engaged.

By 1836 most of these steam locomotives, also sold to other railways in the United Kingdom, had been altered from their original 2-2-0 configuration to a 2-2-2 layout in an effort to improve their running. The data for the Vauxhall-class locomotive, which could pull a useful load at more than 30mph (48km/h), include a tractive effort of about 1,550lb (703kg), two 11 x 18-in (280 x 457-mm) cylinders, driving wheels with a diameter of 5ft 0in (1.524m), steam pressure of about 50lb/sq in (3.5kg/cm²), and overall length of about 24ft 0in (7.315m).

The first steam locomotives made in Germany during 1816 and 1817 were both unsuccessful and as a result it was December 1835 before the first successful steam railway began operation. This was the Ludwigsbahn of Bavaria, linking Nuremberg and Fürth. Approval for the railway had been given by King Ludwig I in the preceding year, and the railway's promoter initially considered the purchase of equipment from Robert Stephenson, but then changed his mind as a result of Stephenson's 'high' price and instead contracted with two citizens of Württemberg for the supply of equipment that they warranted the equal of any British items. The two men then moved to Austria-Hungary and more than doubled the price they wanted so, with the announced date of the railway's opening fast approaching, Herr Scharrer turned to Stephenson for a 2-2-2 locomotive known as Der Adler (The Eagle) and possessing a number of features of the 'Patentee' delivered to the Liverpool & Manchester Railway in 1834. The Patentee was a development of the 'Planet' class with improved axles and wheels.

The success of the Adler is attested by the fact that the Ludwigsbahn operation bought further steam locomotives of the same type, and that the original locomotive was used up to 1857. Details of the Adler are both scarce and in some cases inconsistent, but the most salient data include a tractive effort of 1,220lb (553kg),

fireman had tied down the lever controlling the safety valves to prevent the noise of escaping steam, led finally to the universal adoption of tamper-proof safety valves to prevent any recurrence of this fatal incident. The locomotive was rebuilt with a new boiler and the revised name Phoenix.

Of more overall importance than the Best Friend of Charleston was the Brother Jonathan, a 4-2-0 steam locomotive designed in 1832 by John B. Jervis for another American operator, the Mohawk & Hudson Railroad. This pioneering locomotive introduced the pivoted leading truck (otherwise known as the bogie), which was derived from a notion that Robert Stephenson suggested to Jervis during a visit to England. Originally known as the Experiment, the Brother Jonathan was manufactured at the West Point Foundry. Among its features was a comparatively small boiler, space for the connecting rods between the firebox and the main frames, which were outside the driving wheels, which was fitted to the rear of the firebox. Of these features, it was only the four-wheel truck that became standard as a means of improving guidance round curves, where the outer fore-and-aft pair of truck wheels pressed against the outer rail tangentially, giving all three outer wheels a correct angle of contact on the outer rail of the curve.

The Brother Jonathan had a relatively long and distinguished career in which it

ABOVE LEFT: *The locomotive* Atlantic, *with train built for the Baltimore & Ohio Railroad in 1832.*

ABOVE RIGHT: *The locomotive* Tom Thumb, *built by Peter Cooper for the Baltimore & Ohio Railroad in 1829.*

LEFT: *The locomotive* Hercules *built by Garret & Eastwich of Philadelphia for the Beaver Meadow Railroad, 1837. The locomotive weighed 15 tons.*

OPPOSITE PAGE
LEFT: *Norris' 4-2-0 locomotive, probably of the Birmingham & Gloucester Railway, 1839–42. It was an American-designed*

engine, with front bogie and bar frame. The B&G had 40 of these, made between 1838 and 1840 by Nasmyth in England. Cylinders were around 11¹⁄₂ x 20in (292 x 508mm), boiler pressure circa 55lb/sq in (3.85kg/cm²) and it had four eccentric valve gear.

RIGHT: *Gooch's 0-6-0 Pyracmon locomotive, Great Western Railway, 1847, from an early watercolour. It was a broad-gauge design with 16 x 24-in (406 x 607-mm) cylinders and an inside sandwich frame. Weight was 27¹⁄₂ tons, wheelbase 15ft 5in (4.72m), boiler pressure 115lb/sq in (8kg/cm²) and heating surface 1,373sq ft (127.6m²).*

two 9 x 16-in (229 x 406-mm) cylinders, driving wheels with a diameter of 4ft 6in (1.371m), weight of 31,500lb (14288kg) without tender, and overall length of 25ft 0in (7.62m).

In the U.S.A., Henry Campbell, the engineer of the Philadelphia, Germantown & Norristown Railroad, decided that benefits could accrue from the combination of coupled wheels as pioneered on the *Best Friend of Charleston* and the leading truck of the *Brother Jonathan* to secure a considerable increase in adhesive weight in a steam locomotive that would be able to ride smoothly round curves on tracks that were often very irregularly laid.

The result was the world's first 4-4-0 steam locomotive, which was manufactured in May 1837 by James Brooks and, though in itself designed for coal movement, introduced the most celebrated of all passenger locomotive wheel layouts. The Campbell 4-4-0 locomotive was not in itself successful, being distinctly poor in coping with vertical irregularities in the track. The details for this locomotive include a tractive effort of 4,373lb (1984kg), two 14 x 15.75-in (356 x 400-mm) cylinders, driving wheels with a diameter of 4ft 6in (1.37m), the notably high steam pressure for the period of 90lb/sq in (6.3kg/cm^2), and length of 16ft 5.5in (5.017m).

During 1836, Garret & Eastwich of Philadelphia received an order from the Beaver Meadow Railroad for a 4-4-0 steam locomotive. The company's foreman, Joseph Harrison, knew of the problems of the Campbell 4-4-0 but also remembered the success of the *Brother Jonathan* 4-2-0 locomotive that provided far greater stability through its combination on each side of two driving wheels and the pivot of the leading truck, which provided a type of 'three-legged' stability. Harrison now determined that improved stability could be derived from making the two pairs of driving wheels into a non-swivelling truck through the connection of the axle bearings on each side by a large cast-iron beam that was pivoted at its centre and connected to the main frame of the locomotive by a large leaf spring.

The net effect of this concept was to create a three-point suspension system for an eight-wheel locomotive, a system that fully solved the problem of running on rough tracks and, indeed, was so effective that it was used in steadily more sophisticated form for locomotives up to much later 4-12-2 units.

The resulting locomotive was the *Hercules*, and its success led to the sale of many basically similar locomotives to several railroads and the elevation of Harrison to a partnership in a firm that became Eastwick & Harrison as Garret left it at this time. The details for the *Hercules* included a tractive effort of 4,507lb (2044kg), two 12 x 18-in (305 x 457-mm) cylinders, driving wheels with a diameter of 3ft 8in (1.117m), steam pressure of 90lb/sq in (6.3kg/cm^2), weight of 30,000lb (13608kg) without tender, and length of 18ft 11in (5.766m) without tender.

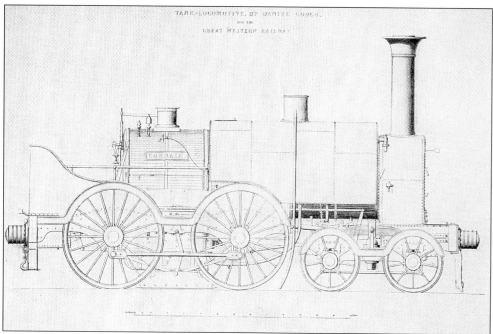

ABOVE: *Daniel Gooch's* Iron Duke *locomotive, Great Western Railway, 1847. From an engraving in Tredgold's* The Steam Engine. *It had a broad-gauge engine with outside sandwich frame. Cylinders were 18 x 24in (457 x 610mm), boiler pressure was originally 100lbsq in (7kg/cm^2), later increased to 115lb/sq in.*

LEFT: *Gooch's 4-4-0* Corsair *saddle-tank locomotive, Great Western Railway, 1849. From D.K. Clark's* Railway Machinery, *1855. It had a broad-gauge engine, cylinders of 17 x 24in (432 x 610mm), wheelbase of 18ft 2in (2.44m) and a weight of 35^3/4 tons. It had inside frames, Gooch's link motion, bogie-class engine and skid-rail brake.*

OPPOSITE ABOVE: *Model of the locomotive* Dorchester *of the Champlain & St. Lawrence Railway, Canada.*

BELOW LEFT: *Bristol station, Great Western Railway, England.*

BELOW RIGHT: *Race between Peter Cooper's locomotive* Tom Thumb *and a horse-drawn railway carriage, Baltimore & Ohio Railroad, 1829.*

With the 'Lafayette' class of 4-2-0 steam locomotives by William Norris, originally for the Baltimore & Ohio Railroad in 1837, the locomotive took a major step toward its definitive form. Originally a draper by trade, Norris had started to build steam locomotives in Philadelphia during 1831 in partnership with Colonel Stephen Long, but then started up on his own and in 1836 produced for the Philadelphia & Columbia Railroad a 4-2-0 locomotive called the *Washington County Farmer*. This was akin to the *Brother Jonathan* in its use of a leading truck, but differed in its use of cylinders outside the wheels and frames, in the nature and arrangement of the valves, and in the location of the driving wheels ahead of rather than behind the firebox to boost the proportion of the engine's weight carried on them.

The success of the *Washington County Farmer* caught the attention of the Baltimore & Ohio Railroad, which by this time had expanded its network to the extent that could no longer be usefully operated by its first-generation 'Grasshopper'-class steam locomotives, and the railroad therefore commissioned a class of eight

locomotives from Norris. The first of these, delivered in 1837, was the *Lafayette*, that was the railroad's first locomotive with a horizontal rather than vertical boiler, although this was used in combination with a circular-section firebox with a notably domed top. The class was very successful, offering higher performance and lower fuel consumption than earlier locomotives, in common with enhanced reliability and simpler maintenance.

In 1837 Norris also completed a similar unit for the Champlain & St. Lawrence Railway in Canada, and this was the first 'modern' locomotive to be exported from the United States, the well proven capabilities of the type then combining with excellent gradient-climbing capability to secure a significant number of other export sales, including a number to Europe, where the first customer was the Vienna-Raab railway, whose *Philadelphia* was shipped late in 1837. Other Norris locomotives went to railways in Brunswick, Prussia and the U.K. Such was the demand for Norris locomotives that the company found it commercially sensible to offer its type in four sizes and therefore weights, differentiated by cylinder bores and grates

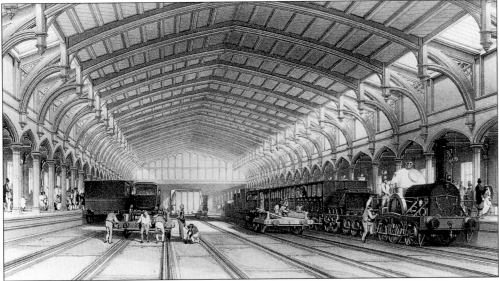

OPPOSITE

CLOCKWISE FROM TOP LEFT: *Central Pacific locomotive No. 82 built by Rogers in 1868. The cordwood piled in the tender is ready for use as fuel. Four-wheeled 15-ft (4.8-m) 'dinky' cabooses like the one shown here were in operation on the Central and Southern Pacific lines.*

There follows a selection of locomotives built by Borsig, including the C-locomotive Isar *for the Warra Railway 1865, the 1B* Gotha *for the Berlin-Stettin Railway 1854, and the 1A1* Beuth *for the Berlin-Anhalter Railway, 1844.*

THIS PAGE, CLOCKWISE FROM TOP LEFT: *More locomotive designs by Borsig which include* Wannsee *for the Berlin-Potsdam-Magdeburg Railway, 1877, the 1B* Moabit *of 1882 and the 1B* Seeve *for the Berlin-Hamburg Railway, 1872–1879.*

of different sizes: the 'A' class had an 11.5in (292mm) bore, the 'A Extra' 12.5in (318mm), the 'B' class 10.5in (268mm) and the 'C' class 9in (229mm).

Locomotives of the Norris type were also widely manufactured in Europe, often without any form of licence. The details for the Lafayette class included a tractive effort of 2,162lb (981kg), two 10.5 x 18-in (268 x 457-mm) cylinders, driving wheels with a

diameter of 4ft 0in (1.219m), steam pressure of 60lb/sq in (4.2kg/cm^2), 2,200lb (998kg) of coke fuel, 540 U.S. gal (450 Imp gal; 2044 litres) of water, total weight of 44,000lb (19958kg), and overall length of 30ft 4.25in (9.25m).

Meanwhile, on the other side of the North Atlantic, momentous events in railway history had begun to unfold with the appointment in 1833 of Isambard Kingdom

Brunel as engineer of the planned Great Western Railway linking the west of England with London. Brunel was not a man to be impressed with current achievements, and one of his earliest decisions was that the gauge of the new railway was to be 7ft 0.25in (2.14m), which was the largest ever adopted for any railway, rather than the figure of 4ft 8.5in (1.432m) selected by the Stephensons and virtually standard in the United Kingdom: in Brunel's opinion, this was the 'coal-wagon gauge'.

Despite the grandiose nature of his plans and his manifest engineering genius, Brunel decided to take no close part in the ordering and design of the locomotives to pull the trains of the Great Western Railway, delegating these tasks to subordinates within the instruction that no six-wheeled locomotive was to exceed 23,520lb (10669kg) in weight with a piston speed of no more than 280ft (85m) per minute. These limits were impossible to attain within a locomotive of practical value, and there is no doubt that its locomotives were the worst features of the Great Western Railway in its earlier days.

Supervising the locomotive fleet was Daniel Gooch, an erstwhile collaborator of the Stephensons, and it was only after a strenuous struggle with Brunel that Gooch was able to persuade the directors of the Great Western Railway to set in hand orders for more than 100 modern six-wheeled locomotives based broadly on the Stephenson Patentee type with layouts such as 2-2-2 for the 62 locomotives required for passenger services and 2-4-0 or 0-6-0 for the other locomotives that were used for freight services.

Unlike the situation which had prevailed previously, in which the manufacturers were given enormous latitude within the sketchiest of guidelines, the situation now controlled by Gooch was far more structured, and the boilers, tenders, moving parts and many other components were common to all the locomotives in an example of standardization on a hitherto unknown scale. Manufacturers received not only drawings but also templates, and were also made financially responsible for all repairs required within the first 1,000 miles (1609km) of any locomotive's operation with its planned full load.

The first of the new passenger locomotives, delivered in March 1840, was the *Fire Fly*, manufactured by Jones, Turner & Evans of Newton-le-Willows in Lancashire. Later units of the same basic

class from the same manufacturer were the *Spit Fire, Wild Fire, Fire Ball, Fire King* and *Fire Brand*. The capabilities of the new class were revealed on 17 March 1840, when the *Fire Fly* pulled a special train over a 30.75-mile (49.5-km) distance at an average of just under 50mph (80.5km/h) and reached a maximum speed of 58mph (93km/h). By the end of 1840, for the opening to Wootton Bassett beyond Swindon, a further 25 of these locomotives were available and a timetable worthy of the name could be issued at last.

By December 1842 another 56 of the

locomotives had been delivered by another six manufacturers, and the last of the series was not withdrawn from service until 1879. The details of the 'Fire Fly' class included a tractive effort of 2,049lb (929kg), two 15 x 18-in (381 x 457-mm) cylinders, driving wheels with a diameter of 7ft 0in (2.134m), steam pressure of 50lb/sq in (3.5kg/cm^2), 3,400lb (1542kg) of coke fuel, 2,160 U.S. gal (1,800 Imp gal; 8183 litres) of water, total weight of 92,500lb (41958kg), and overall length of 39ft 4in (11.989m).

In 1841 the locomotive-building industry began to come of age in Germany

Here, circa 1895, Boston & Maine's American Standard-class locomotive (No. 150) has just moved out of the Danvers, Massachusetts engine house.

as three manufacturers each delivered their first offerings: these manufacturers were Borsig of Berlin, Maffei of Munich and Emil Kessler of Karlsruhe. At the time of Borsig's expansion from several other enterprises into locomotive manufacture, the Norris 4-2-0 locomotives were very popular in European circles, and Borsig's first

ABOVE LEFT: *Central Pacific Railroad's locomotive* Jupiter *with bandsmen of the 21st Infantry, stationed at Fort Douglas, Utah, at the completion of the transcontinental railway at Promontory, Utah on 10 May 1869.*

ABOVE RIGHT: *Train on one of the Bollman truss bridges on the Maryland North Branch of the Baltimore & Ohio Railroad. The train ran between Baltimore and Wheeling and back, carrying 40 photographers and artists making frequent stops so that they could photograph and paint. 1858.*

LEFT: *A one-car Northern Pacific train, with wood-burning balloon stack locomotive is shown at the end of the bridge over the Missouri between Bismarck and Mandan, Dakota Territory, in 1882.*

locomotives were 15 similar units delivered to the Berlin-Anhalter railway company. Though modelled closely on the American original, the German locomotive had several Borsig improvements. The type was very successful and soon attracted additional orders.

Within a period of two years Borsig had added further improvements, some of its own design and others derived from British ideas. The blend of an American core design with German and British improvements was highly attractive, and was fully evident in the *Beuth*, a 2-2-2 locomotive delivered to the Berlin-Anhalter railway in 1843. The equal spacing of the three axles offered a better distribution of weight than in the Norris 4-2-0 type, and the new valves (based on a type developed by William Howe of the Stephenson company) were so good that they became virtually standard for all steam locomotives over the next 60 years.

The *Beuth* was the 24th locomotive manufactured by Borsig, and its success attracted a relative flood of orders to the extent that by 1846 Borsig had completed no fewer than 120 locomotives. The details of the *Beuth* included a tractive effort of 4,123lb (1870kg), two 13.1 x 22.3-in (333 x 566-mm) cylinders, driving wheels with a diameter of 5ft 0.75in (1.543m), steam pressure of 78lb/sq in (5.5kg/cm²), weight of 40,785lb (18500kg) without tender, and length of 20ft 2in (6.143m) without tender.

An exact French contemporary of the *Beuth* was the 'Buddicom' class of 2-2-2 steam locomotives designed for the Paris-Rouen railway by W. B. Buddicom, one of many British engineers who took the ideas of the Stephensons round the world and, in this instance, improved upon them. The Buddicom class of 2-2-2 locomotives was a further step (rivalled by the 'Crew' class designed in the U.K. by Alexander Allan) in the development of European locomotives from the *Northumbrian* toward what became established as the norm with two outside cylinders.

The spur to the creation of the new design was the tendency of the cranked axles of inside-cylinder locomotives to breakage and, as well as adopting outside cylinders, the Buddicom-class design also had the new type of Stephenson link motion and a deep firebox between the two rear wheels. The Buddicom class was very effective, and was built in moderately large

numbers including 22 that were later converted to 2-2-2 tank locomotive standard. The details of the Buddicom class included a tractive effort of 3,219lb (1460kg), two 12.5 x 21-in (318 x 533-mm) cylinders, driving wheels with a diameter of 5ft 3in (1.60m), and steam pressure of 70lb/sq in (5kg/cm²).

During 1836 John Haswell, a Scotsman, travelled to Austria-Hungary to supervise the entry into service of some locomotives bought from the U.K. With this task satisfactorily completed, Haswell was invited to remain in the country as the head of the locomotive element of the short line linking Vienna and Gloggnitz. Haswell

remained in Austria-Hungary to the time of his death in 1897, and among his steam locomotive designs was the 'Gloggnitzer' class of 4-4-0 units based on the Norris type and used mainly on the extension of the Gloggnitz line to Laibach (now Ljubljana) over the Semmering Pass.

The Gloggnitz class had a number of unusual features, including the ability of the leading truck to move radially rather than just pivot round its centre as on the original Norris design, a change made desirable by the location of the coupled driving wheels close to the truck, which exercised a measure of constraint on the locomotive's axis and therefore made it important that the

truck should possess a measure of lateral displacement capability. The details of the Gloggnitzer-class locomotive included a tractive effort of 5,754lb (2610kg), two 14.5 x 23-in (368 x 584-mm) cylinders, driving wheels with a diameter of 4ft 7.75in (1.42m), steam pressure of 78lb/sq in (5.5kg/cm²), 4,409lb (2000kg) of fuel, 1,796 U.S. gal (1,496 Imp gal; 6800 litres) of water, total weight of 70,547lb (32000kg), and overall length of 42ft 2in (12.853m).

Manufactured by Thomas Rogers of Paterson, New Jersey, during 1855, the *General* remains a classic example of the 'American Standard' class of 4-4-0 steam locomotives, which was arguably the most

OPPOSITE: Golden Spike National Monument replicas of Central Pacific 4-4-0 Jupiter *and Union Pacific No. 119 at Promontory Point, Utah.*

RIGHT: *Steam locomotives, run on a variety of gauges, have a long and proud tradition in India.*

numerous and successful locomotive design ever created. It was Rogers who was largely responsible for introducing to American practice most of the features which made the true American Standard class. The most important of these was the Stephenson link motion, which permitted the expansive use of steam, and was used in place of the 'gab' or 'hook' reversing gears used up to that time and provided only 'full forward' and 'full backward' positions. Rogers otherwise concentrated on good proportions and excellence of detail rather than innovation as such.

To provide a measure of flexibility on tighter curves, early American Standard locomotives had the same type of flangeless forward driving wheels as their predecessors, but by the late 1850s the leading truck instead had provision for lateral movement to yield the same effect. The use of wood rather than coal was extremely common in the first part of the career of the American Standard locomotives, and as a result there were a wide assortment of spark-catching smokestacks in an effort to reduce the possibility of a spark flying off to the side of the track and setting fire to woods or crops.

By the late 1850s, generally similar locomotives were being made by other manufacturers including Baldwin, Brooks Mason, Danforth, Grant, and Hinkley began offering similar locomotives, which generally operated on the roughly laid tracks of the period at an average speed of about 25mph (40km/h). The American Standard had a relatively long life, the need to pull longer and heavier loads meant that by the 1880s the original type had often been supplemented if not supplanted by larger steam locomotives using the same 4-4-0 configuration or alternatively the 4-6-0 layout. About 25,000 of these classic locomotives were built to a standard that was notable for its general uniformity in all but detail. The American Standard was the first and possibly the only 'universal locomotive', and the main difference between the units built to pull passenger trains and those intended for the freight market was the large diameter of the former's driving wheels, 5ft 6in (1.676m) as compared with 5ft 0in (1.524m).

Some of the locomotives survived in useful American service into the 1950s, and the details of the *General* include a tractive effort of 6,885lb (3123kg), two 15 x 24-in (381 x 610-mm) cylinders, driving wheels with a diameter of 5ft 0in (1.524m), steam pressure of 90lb/sq in (6.35kg/cm^2), 2,000 U.S. gal (1,665 Imp gal; 7571 litres) of water, total weight of 90,000lb (40824kg) and overall length of 52ft 3in (15.926m).

The 'Problem' or 'Lady of the Lake' class of 2-2-2 steam locomotives, designed by John Ramsbottom and introduced to British service by the London & North Western Railway during 1859, remained in useful 'first-line' service for nearly 50 years, which was a considerable achievement in its own right and all the more so for a class introduced at a time that locomotive technology was still developing relatively quickly.

The primary advantage enjoyed by the Problem class, as indeed with all of the great steam locomotives right up to the present, was a total avoidance of complexity: the class had no trucks, for example, the leading axle being carried in the frames like the others, the valve arrangement for the outside cylinders was simplicity itself, and after the first ten a simple injector system was used in place of pumps to top up the boiler.

The General Lowell, *an American Standard-type 4-4-0 locomotive, photographed at Burlington, Iowa during the late Civil War period. The engine was named for Brigadier-General Charles Lowell, Jnr., killed at the battle of Cedar Creek on 19 October 1864. Lowell had been assistant treasurer and land agent of the fledgling Burlington & Missouri River Railroad from its earliest days until he resigned on 25 October 1860 to become an ironmaker at Mt. Savage, Maryland. He was replaced by his assistant, 19-year-old Charles E. Perkins, who later became president of the Chicago, Burlington & Quincy Railroad.*

One of the most notable tasks undertaken by the locomotives of the Problem class was the haulage of the *Irish Mail* between Euston in London and Holyhead on Anglesey, the locomotive being changed at Stafford. A retrograde step occurred in 1871 when Ramsbottom was succeeded by Francis Webb, who unfortunately believed in complexity. This gave rise to a number of complex and highly unreliable compound locomotives. The compound locomotives that resulted were not as reliable as they should have been, and this led to a renewed demand for the services of the now-elderly Problem-class locomotives, which were largely rebuilt in the 1890s with greater weight in addition to the crew cabs that had been added during an

earlier rebuild programme. The details for the Problem-class locomotives in their final form included a tractive effort of 9,827lb (4458kg), two 16 x 24-in (406 x 610-mm) cylinders, driving wheels with a diameter of 7ft 9in (2.324m), steam pressure of 150lb/sq in (10.5kg/cm²), 2,162 U.S. gal (1,800 Imp gal; 8183 litres) of water, total weight of 133,000lb (60329kg), and overall length of 43ft 8in (13.31m).

Gallic flair was evident in a number of French steam locomotive designs, but in none more so than the '121' class that entered service in 1876 on the *Route Impériale* of the Paris, Lyons & Mediterranean railway. Needing locomotives of greater power than the Crampton 4-2-0 units it was currently

operating, the railway initially produced from 1868 some 50 long-boiler 2-4-0 locomotives and then searched for still more power for this prestigious but arduous service between the French capital and the Mediterranean coast. This led to the 121 class of an initial 60 (but ultimately 400 by 1883) locomotives with a 2-4-2 layout, and all of the earlier long-boiler locomotives were then rebuilt to this standard for increased stability.

Further improvement was introduced in 1888, when work was started on another batch of 2-4-2 locomotives, which must be regarded as one of the high points in French steam locomotive design. Only 10 per cent heavier than the originals, these final units introduced three definitive features in the

form of the Walschaert valve gear (later standard all over the world), a boiler designed for a pressure of 214lb/sq in (15kg/cm²) that was a 65 per cent increase over the boiler pressure of the parent design, and a switch from simple to compound operation for much enhanced thermal efficiency to increase the ratio between the power produced and the fuel burned.

The details for the middle tranche of 121-class locomotives included a tractive effort of 12,224lb (5545kg), two 19.7 x 23.7-in (500 x 650-mm) cylinders, driving wheels with a diameter of 6ft 10.75in (2.10m), steam pressure of 129lb/sq in (9kg/cm²), weight of 109,568lb (49700kg) with tender, and length of 56ft 5.75in (17.215m) without tender.

LEFT: *Union Pacific's locomotive No. 574 (4-4-0) heading a passenger train at Genoa, Nebraska. The engineer is H.A. Riley, fireman E.P. Rogers, conductor Harry Schaffer and breakman W.F. McFadden.*

BELOW: *Three switch engines and their crews pose in front of the former station at Pacific Junction, Iowa, in 1905. This is where the Kansas City-Council Bluffs line crosses the main line to Lincoln and where trains for Council Bluffs and Omaha can turn north and follow the Missouri. The one on the left is an E-class, No. 1390 is in the centre and No. 1423 on the right is a G-class engine.*

It had been a matter of faith since the Patentee class of 2-2-2 locomotives that 'high-speed' rail travel demanded that the locomotive needed smaller guide wheels ahead of the larger driving wheels, but in 1882 the London, Brighton & South Coast Railway introduced the 'Gladstone' class of 0-4-2 locomotives that were initially regarded with more than a touch of suspicion by the 'experts' of the time. Experience soon revealed, however, that William Stroudley was right to dispense with the guiding wheels, as the Gladstone-class locomotives behaved impeccably and were, moreover, extremely attractive and economical to run. As a result, Stroudley is one of the comparative handful of designers whose locomotives have enjoyed a career of 70 years or more.

Production of the Gladstone class amounted to 36 locomotives, the last of them completed in 1890, and the success of the type can be attributed mostly to its basically simple design, which resulted in good working and considerable reliability, and the careful arrangement of the suspension arrangements with leaf springs on the leading axle and more 'giving' coil springs on the centre axle. Stroudley was not a believer in too great an emphasis on simplicity when a measure of complexity could provide dividends, however, and as a result the Gladstone-class locomotives included a system to condense the exhaust steam into the feed water, in the process recovering some of the heat that would

otherwise have been wasted, and the use of air-driven assistance (using air from the Westinghouse air-brake supply) for the screw reversing gear. The details of the Gladstone-class locomotive included a tractive effort of 13,211lb (5993kg), two 18.25 x 26-in (464 x 660-mm) cylinders, driving wheels with a diameter of 6ft 6in (1.981m), steam pressure of 140lb/sq in (9.8kg/cm²), 9,000lb (4082kg) of fuel, 2,690 U.S. gal (2,240 Imp gal; 10183 litres) of water, total weight of 153,000lb (69401kg), and overall length of 51ft 10in (15.80m).

Designed by Daniel Gooch and introduced in 1888 on the wide-gauge lines of the Great Western Railway, the 'Rover' class of 4-2-2 steam locomotives were the successors of the Fire Fly class of 2-2-2 locomotives. The prototype for the class, which resulted from a process of continuous refinement, was the *Great Western* that

appeared in 1846 as what was in effect a stretched version of the Fire Fly class with greater grate area and tractive power at the expense of a weight increase of one-fifth. This was too much for the 2-2-2 layout, and after it had suffered a broken front axle soon after completion, the *Great Western* was revised to a 4-2-2 layout with the leading pair of wheels supported by the frames rather than attached to a pivoted truck. In this form the design was good, and there followed a series of steadily improved subclasses that provided the backbone of the Great Western Railway's fleet of locomotives.

The final subclass was the 'Rover' class, of which 54 were built with details that included a tractive effort of 9,640lb (4373kg), two 18 x 24-in (457 x 610-mm) cylinders, driving wheels with a diameter of 8ft 0in (2.438m), steam pressure 140lb/sq in (9.8kg/cm²), 7,000lb (3175kg) of fuel, 3,603

U.S. gal (3,000 Imp gal; 13638 litres) of water, total weight of 160,000lb (72576kg), and overall length of 47ft 6in (14.478m).

With the 'S3' class of 4-4-0 steam locomotives built for the Royal Prussian Union railway from 1893, a thoroughly modern look reached Germany's rail network, which was fast approaching its definitive primary form. The predecessors of the S3-class locomotives in the 1880s were a series of 2-4-0 locomotives with outside cylinders, but at this time there were passenger demands for higher levels of comfort and greater speeds, and the implementation of these constraints demanded the introduction of larger locomotives to provide the power required for what must inevitably be heavier trains. The superintendent of locomotives at Hanover was at the time August von Berries, who was despatched on a tour of the U.K.

ABOVE LEFT: Locomotive No. 999 4-4-0 of the New York Central Railroad's Empire State Express.

ABOVE: Locomotive No. 810 4-6-0 of the Boston & Maine Railroad poses at Boston's Old North Station shortly after the B&M had leased the Concorde & Montreal Railroad, 1895.

OPPOSITE
ABOVE: LNWR Ramsbottom Problem 2-2-2 Prince Alfred at Bletchley Station, Buckinghamshire, England, circa 1900.

BELOW LEFT: The first passenger station in Minneapolis, photographed in 1873. The St. Paul & Pacific Railroad was the first in the north-west, and ran from St. Paul to Minneapolis.

BELOW RIGHT: Depot of the U.S. Military Railroad at City Point, Virginia.

and the U.S.A. with the brief of assessing the latest locomotive thinking in these countries. The result was the decision that the larger boiler required for the generation of the desired power would require the introduction of another axle to create the 4-4-0 arrangement that was so successful in the U.S.A.

During 1890 the Henschel company manufactured two 4-4-0 locomotives with a two-cylinder compound-propulsion arrangement to a design by von Borries, and in the succeeding year Henschel constructed another four 4-4-0 locomotives (two each with compound- and simple-expansion propulsion) to the design of Lochner, the superintendent of locomotives at Erfurt. Lochner's simple-expansion system was deemed most effective, and there followed 150 locomotives before a reconsideration of the matter led to the decision that the von

LEFT: *LNWR Ramsbottom Problem-class 2-2-2* Tornado *at Carlisle, England in 1899.*

OPPOSITE
ABOVE LEFT: *Locomotive No. 101 Central Vermont,* Burlington Northern Railroad.

ABOVE RIGHT: *Western Railway's* Dragon *locomotive.*

BELOW LEFT: *Great Northern Railway Stirling 8-ft single No. 547, built in 1878. (Photographed circa 1905.)*

BELOW RIGHT: *Boston & Maine's 4-4-0 locomotive No. 53 on the turntable at the Charleston, Massachusetts engine house, circa 1910.*

Berries type of compound propulsion offered advantages. During 1892 August von Berries therefore designed an improved version of his original concept as the S3 design in which the letter stood for *schnellzuglokomotiv* (express locomotive). The type was extremely effective, and 1,073 such locomotives were therefore manufactured between 1892 and 1904 as 1,027 for the Prussian and 46 for other German state railways. Another 424 locomotives with smaller driving wheels

were also constructed as 'P4'-class units.

The S3 class was notable not only for its considerable size, but also for the fact that it was the first locomotive class to make use of steam superheating. The attraction of superheating results from the fact that water evaporates to steam at a specific temperature dependent on the ambient pressure: at the 171-lb/sq in (12-kg/cm²) working pressure of the S3 class, this temperature is 376°F (191°C) and when there is water in the boiler the steam

temperature cannot rise above that of the water. As the steam leaves the boiler it takes particles of water with it, and coming into contact with the cooler metal of the steam pipes, valves, cylinders and pistons it starts to lose its heat, part of it condensing into water to supplement the water droplets already being precipitated from the steam. Most of the work effected on the piston results from the expansion of the steam after the closure of the valve, but as water has no capacity for expansion, its presence in the

cylinder is a waste, and so too therefore is the energy used to heat it in the boiler.

However, the further heating of the steam after its departure from the boiler, and therefore no longer in contact with the temperature-limiting volume of water still in the boiler, allows the particles of water in the steam to be evaporated, in the process drying the steam and further increasing its volume. Additional heat raises the temperature of the dry steam, making it superheated. The slight cooling of

TOP: Paris, Lyons & Mediterranean LM 2-4-2 locomotive No. 85, of which 400 were built.

TOP RIGHT: Locomotive No. C 169 built 1898–1901 for the famous Route Impériale *of the Paris, Lyons & Mediterranean railway.*

ABOVE: LNWR Webb Teutonic-compound 2-2-2-0 1304 Jeanie Deans.

superheated steam as it touches the walls of the cylinder etc. does not cause condensation until all the superheat has been removed. Superheating therefore removes the possibility of condensation in the cylinder, thereby allowing better use to be made of the energy locked into the steam's heat.

The advantages of superheating had been appreciated for some time, but it was only in the 1890s that there appeared the first workable superheater designs, of which the most significant was that of Dr. Wilhelm Schmidt of Kassel. This was based on the ducting of the steam (between the boiler and the header that distributed the steam to the two cylinders) into a number of small tubes enclosed in a large-diameter tube through which flames from the firebox were ducted to create the superheating effect.

The Schmidt superheater was evaluated in single S3- and P4-class locomotives adapted in 1898 and proved generally successful except for the distortion of the

superheater's outside cylinder as a result of the heat of the flames inside it. Schmidt therefore revised his concept to use the cooler but still high temperature of the smokebox, and this proved wholly successful. In 1899 two S3-class locomotives were completed with the definitive Schmidt smokebox type of superheater, and the success of the system was attested by a 12 per cent reduction in fuel consumption. The system soon became standard for all new locomotives of the larger, high-speed type, further refinement of the concept resulting in fuel economies of up to 20 per cent.

So successful were the superheated S3-class locomotives that 34 were still in service when the unified German rail network was created in 1924. The details of the S3 class included one 18.9 x 23.6-in (480 x 600-mm) high-pressure cylinder and one 26.6 x 23.6-in (680 x 600-mm) low-pressure cylinder, driving wheels with a

RIGHT: Class D16/3 No.62618 resplendent in fully lined apple green, with the first British Rail symbol (a very rare combination), heads a Cambridge train out of Colchester, England in the summer of 1950/51.One of the last series of the Claud Hamilton class built by the LNER in 1923, it retained the decorative valancing when converted to a D16/3 in 1944.

BELOW: A line-up of Santa Fe history from left to right: locomotive *Cyrus K.* Holliday, *No. 3767, No. 3460* Blue Goose, *diesel freight and diesel passenger locomotives.*

diameter of 6ft 6in (1.98m), steam pressure of 171lb/sq in (12kg/cm²), 11,023lb (5000kg) of fuel, 5,680 U.S. gal (4,729 Imp gal; 21500 litres) of water, weight of 111,993lb (50800kg) without tender, and overall length of 57ft 7in (17.56m).

Although the American Standard class of 4-4-0 steam locomotives performed notably as the main passenger-hauling locomotive of the U.S. railroad networks from the 1850s, by the 1880s it had become clear that the movement of heavier trains at higher speeds on the technically more sophisticated railroads of the states of the U.S.A.'s eastern seaboard required larger and more powerful locomotives, generally of

the 4-6-0 configuration created by the simple expedient of adding a third coupled axle to the rear of the axles for the two current pairs of driving wheels and 'streamlining' the whole unit both internally and externally. These alterations were not without their problems, but even so some 16,000 such locomotives were manufactured in the period between 1880 and 1910.

Typical of this impressive breed was the 'I-1' class made by the Brooks Locomotive Works of Dunkirk in New York during 1900 for the Lake Shore & Michigan Southern Railroad, which needed a type to pull the prestige trains on the western section of the rail line (linking New York on the U.S.A.'s eastern coast and Chicago in Illinois on the south coast of Lake Michigan) of what was soon the New York Central Railroad. The locomotives performed well, pulling heavy five-coach trains at moderately high speeds with a smooth ride, including the classic *Twentieth Century Limited* de-luxe service introduced in June 1902, but fell out of favour when the increase in passenger loads from the beginning of the 20th century required more power than could sensibly be delivered by a derivative of the American Standard class. The details of the I-1 class included a tractive effort of 23,800lb (10796kg), two 20 x 28-in (508 x 711-mm) cylinders, driving wheels with a diameter of 6ft 10in (2.032m), steam pressure of 200lb/sq in (14.1kg/cm²), 17,500lb (7938kg) of fuel, 7,200 U.S. gal (5,995 Imp gal; 27255 litres) of water, total weight of 300,000lb (136080kg), and overall length of 62ft 3in (18.914m).

One of the first in overall terms and one of the most important operators in the U.S.A., the Pennsylvania Railroad had by the end of the 19th century become widely known for its large and powerful locomotives, most of them manufactured in the company's own facilities at Altoona. Typical of this breed were the 4-4-0 steam locomotives produced in several classes on which the most important and successful was the 'D16' class that first appeared in 1895 and was later recognized as one of the high points in the design and manufacture of American steam locomotives.

The class was typified by large cylinders and a boiler that operated at a high pressure by the standards of the period, and it was also notable in purely visual terms for the considerable height of its boiler, which resulted from the installation of the firebox above rather than between the frames.

The class was initially manufactured in two variants, namely the 'D16a' class with driving wheels of 6ft 10in (2.032m) diameter for operation on the railroad's flatter routes, and the D16 proper with driving wheels of 5ft 8in (1.727m) diameter for operation on the railroad's less flat routes. The D16a class was soon known for its high speed, and operated on the 58-mile (93-km) 'racetrack' between Camden and Atlantic City on which the Pennsylvania Railroad vied directly with the Atlantic City Railroad.

The D16 class was built to the extent of 426 locomotives in five subclasses in the period between 1895 and 1910. In the first years of the 20th century the locomotives of the D16 classes were generally outdone by

OPPOSITE

ABOVE: *The K4-class 4-6-2 locomotives were the mainstay of steam operations for the Pennsylvania Railroad until after World War II.*

BELOW: *Great Eastern Railway Claud Hamilton-class 4-4-0.*

ABOVE: *Class L Mallet-articulated. Great Northern's L-class 2-6-6-2 locomotives, built by Baldwin in 1906–07, were true Mallets. No.1810, shown here, was an L-2 of 1907 vintage.*

ABOVE RIGHT: *Pennsylvania Railroad 4-4-2 with slide valves, crossing the Skilkill river bridge.*

RIGHT: *The Great Eastern Railway Claud Hamilton-class 4-4-0 locomotive was named for the chairman of the company and came into being at the turn of the century.*

the newer 'Atlantic'- and 'Pacific'-class locomotives in terms of power and therefore performance, but from 1914 just under half of the D16-class locomotives were considerably updated to the 'D16sb' class standard with a number of improvements including cylinders enlarged from the original 18.5 x 26-in (470 x 660-mm) type, and a Schmidt superheating system. In this form the locomotives became important on branch lines, some of them remaining in service until the early 1940s. The details for the D16sb-class locomotive included a tractive effort of 23,900lb (10841kg), two 20.5 x 26-in (521 x 660-mm) driving wheels with a diameter of 5ft 8in (1.727m), steam pressure of 175lb/sq in (12.3kg/cm^2), 26,000lb (11794kg) of fuel, 5,600 U.S. gal (4,663 Imp gal; 21198 litres) of water, total weight of 281,000lb (127462kg), and overall length of 67ft 0in (20.422m).

As noted above, there was intense rivalry between the Pennsylvania Railroad and the Atlantic City Railroad in those regions near Atlantic City in New Jersey where the two operators' networks overlapped, and each tried to secure the lion's share of the traffic between the heavily populated inland cities round Philadelphia and the coastal resorts of New Jersey. This rivalry consisted not of the provision of additional capacity at peak periods, mainly July and August of each year, but in the provision of the fastest services with as much time as possible trimmed from the scheduled journey through regular running at speeds in excess of 90mph (145km/h) for an average journey speed of 70mph (113km/h) or more.

One of the key instruments in the effort by the Atlantic City Railroad from the last years of the 19th century into the first years of the 20th century was the 'Camelback' class of 4-4-2 locomotives, which had an unusual appearance in that they seemed to be squashed longitudinally, but introduced a number of important features. These last included a firebox that was both wide and deep, allowing the effective burning of anthracite coal and, as it was later found, bituminous coal and then oil. Other features that made the class notable were pairs of compound cylinders on each side with drive

by means of a common cross head, and the 'camelback' cab for the driver, who was thus carried over the boiler, while the fireman was provided with only the most rudimentary protection in the normal location at the rear of the locomotive. The arrangement certainly gave the driver a good field of vision, but made communication between the driver and fireman extremely difficult.

At the technical level the Camelback class was successful, and was therefore built in moderately large numbers for the Atlantic City Railroad (soon the Philadelphia & Reading Railroad). Several

OPPOSITE: An early passenger train of the late 1880s or 1890s, probably taken between Great Falls and Butte on the line of the Montana Central Railway. The Montana Central became part of the Great Northern Railway.

THIS PAGE
ABOVE: Winans' Camel *locomotive No. 65, built by Ross Winans in Baltimore in 1850.*

RIGHT: The Italian locomotive Dante Alighieri, *built by Henschel and Son in 1873.*

other railroads on the east coast of the U.S.A. also built locomotives of the same basic concept. The details of the Camelback class included a tractive effort of 22,906lb (10390kg), two 13 x 26-in (330 x 660-mm) high-pressure cylinders and two 22 x 26-in (559 x 660-mm) low-pressure cylinders, driving wheels with a diameter of 7ft 0in (2.134m), steam pressure of 200lb/sq in (14kg/cm²), 4,000 U.S. gal (3,331 Imp gal; 15142 litres) of water, and total weight of 218,000lb (98885kg),

By the end of the 19th century the 'standard' American steam locomotive for use on passenger services was of the 4-4-0 configuration, but by this time it was clear that further progress in terms of hauling ability and speed demanded a configuration with more than eight wheels. As a result, there emerged a number of 10-wheel designs divided neatly into the 4-6-0 and 4-4-2 layouts. The former type offered greater adhesive weight (the weight on the driving wheels) but was limited by the area of the grate that could be installed between the rear pair of driving wheels, while the latter (later known as the 'Atlantic' type) had lesser adhesive weight but could be fitted with a larger grate between the undriven rear wheels.

The Pennsylvania Railroad almost inevitably adopted the Atlantic type of locomotive as it already possessed the network of heavier track capable of accepting this type's heavy axle loads, and at the technical level wanted to be able to burn large quantities of modest-quality coal rather than smaller quantities of a higher grade.

First manufactured in the railroad's Altoona facility in 1899, the first two Atlantic-type locomotives had a grate area of 68sq ft (6.32m²), which was more than twice the figure for any of the railroad's 4-4-0 locomotives. A third locomotive had the smaller grate area of 55.5sq ft (5.16m²), and it was this size that became standard for all later Atlantic-type locomotives, which totalled 576 in a number of subclasses. The 'E2' class had cylinders with a diameter of 20.5in (521mm) while the cylinders of the 'E3' class, intended mainly for heavier work, had a diameter of 22in (559mm).

By 1913, manufacture of the Atlantic type had reached 493 units, and it seemed that the type had reached the limit of its development in the face of competition from the more modern 'Pacific' type with its three pairs of coupled driving wheels. It was just before this stage, though, that Axel Vogt, the

ABOVE: No. 2561 Minoru *on an East Coast express, England in August 1932.*

RIGHT: The former New Zealand Railway's A-class 0-4-0 tank locomotive of 1873 departs with a 1st Plains Branch Railway train.

OPPOSITE
ABOVE LEFT: A typical mixed train headed by an old J-class dating from the 1870s at Dunsandel station near Canterbury, New Zealand, early 1900s.

ABOVE RIGHT: Manchester Locomotive Works 4-4-0 locomotive No. 31 on the Fitchburg Railroad. It was leased by Boston & Maine from 1 July 1900.

BELOW: In their day, Claud Hamilton-class 4-4-0 locomotives were the expresses of the Great Eastern Railway.

railroad's chief engineer, had decided that the driving-wheel arrangement of the Pacific type was unnecessarily complex and planned a further-improved version of the Atlantic type with a boiler increased in maximum diameter from 5ft 5.5in (1.664m) to 6ft 4.75in (1.949m) and with a combustion chamber at the front.

The prototype of this 'E6' class of locomotives first appeared in 1910 and revealed greater power than the Pacific type at higher speeds. Two more locomotives were then made with a superheating system, allowing a further increase in cylinder diameter of 23.5in (597mm), and these locomotives revealed excellent performance. There followed production of 80 E6-class locomotives, all completed between February and August 1914 to become the mainstays of the Pennsylvania Railroad's express services on flatter parts of its route network. After the advent of the definitive 'K4' class of Pacific-type locomotives after the end of World War I in 1918, the E6-class locomotives were gradually relegated to

lesser services. Many of the earlier locomotives were upgraded over the years with features such as superheating, five of them lasting in service to 1947. The details for the 'E3sd' subclass included a tractive effort of 27,400lb (12429kg), two 22 x 26-in (559 x 660-mm) cylinders, driving wheels with a diameter of 6ft 8in (2.032m), steam pressure of 205lb/sq in (14.4kg/cm^2), 34,200lb (15513kg) of fuel, 6,800 U.S. gal (5,662 Imp gal; 25741 litres) of water, total weight of 363,500lb (164884kg), and overall length of 71ft 6in (21.640m).

Back on the eastern side of the North Atlantic Ocean, January 1900 saw the appearance of the first of the 'Claud Hamilton' class of 4-4-0 locomotives named for the chairman of the company that built it, the Great Eastern Railway. Though its inside-cylinder layout was typical of the previous century, the way ahead was presaged in features such as the large cab with four big side windows, the power-operated reversing gear, water scoop, and provision for the burning of waste oil products (a by-product of the company's oil-gas operation) rather than coal. Good features that were not quite as advanced included an exhaust steam injector and a variable-nozzle blast pipe.

The history of the Claud Hamilton class was complex, and eventually extended to cover a total of 121 such locomotives built in the period between 1900 and 1923 in a number of subclasses characterized by the introduction of features such as larger boilers, a superheating system, and piston rather than slide valves. All these features were built into the definitive 'Super Claud' class of which 10 were completed. As new-build locomotives introduced improved features, most of the older units were rebuilt to the improved standard, most of them by the London & North Eastern Railway that introduced its own designation system. In overall terms, therefore, there were 41 of the original Claud Hamilton (LNER 'D14') class locomotives that served up to 1931 and underwent no rebuilds, 66 of what later became the 'D15' class (nine rebuilt) that served between 1903 and 1933 and introduced the Belpaire firebox, four of what later became the 'D15/1' (70 rebuilt) class that served between 1911 and 1935 and introduced the superheating system, none of what became the 'D15/2' class (80 rebuilt) that served between 1914 and 1952 and introduced a lengthened smokebox, 10 of the 'Super Claud' or later 'D16/1' class (five rebuilt) that served between 1923 and 1934 and introduced a larger boiler, none of the 'D16/2' class (40 rebuilt) that served between 1926 and 1952 and were basically

OPPOSITE
ABOVE LEFT: *The 232 Nord railway Baltic-class locomotive, No. 1102.*

ABOVE RIGHT: *Locomotive No. 8 with F15 Pacific No. 434 charges along with four cars of train, east of Russell, Kentucky in June 1947.*

BELOW: *An Auckland-Wellington express headed by a 'K'-class 4-8-4 locomotive No. 905 between Taupiri and Ngaruawahia in the Waikato district, 7 March 1952.*

THIS PAGE
ABOVE: *Nord 4-4-2 de Glehn compound.*

RIGHT: *New Zealand Railways Q-class 4-6-2 locomotive No. 346 at the Oamaru locomotive depot when it was used for hauling passenger trains over the steeply-graded section of line between Oamaru and Dunedin, South Island, New Zealand.*

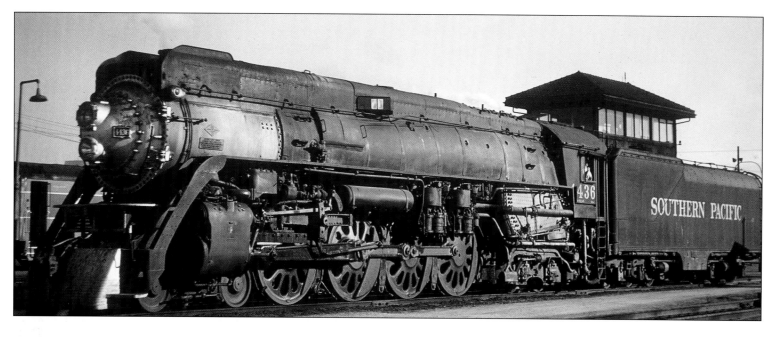

LEFT: Southern Pacific Railroad 4-8-4 No. 4436 at San Francisco, July 1952.

BELOW LEFT: Union Pacific 4-8-4 on a northbound evening passenger service at Denver, Colorado, July 1952.

BELOW: LNER Gresley Pacific No. 4479 Robert the Devil at Doncaster, England in 1935.

OPPOSITE: Norfolk & Western Railroad 'J'-class 4-8-4 No. 609 on a westbound passenger train.

similar to the 'D16/1' class units, and none of the 'D16/3' class (104 rebuilt) that served between 1033 and 1958 and saw the removal of the coupling rod splashers and the reintroduction of round-topped boilers.

The details of the Claud Hamilton class, of which all (13, 16 and 88 examples of the D15/2, D16/2 and D16/3 classes respectively) were still in service at the time of the nationalization of the British rail system on the first day of 1948, included a tractive effort of 17,100lb (7757kg), two 19 x 26-in (483 x 660-mm) cylinders, driving wheels with a diameter of 7ft 0in (2.134m), steam pressure of 180lb/sq in (12.7kg/cm²), 859 U.S. gal (715 Imp gal; 3250 litres) of oil fuel, 4,143 U.S. gal (3,450 Imp gal; 15864 litres) of water, total weight of 213,000lb (96617kg), and overall length of 53ft 4.75in (16.276m).

Alfred de Glehn was English but became the chief engineer of the Société Alsacienne de Constructions Mécaniques during the 1870s before he reached the age of 30, and with Gaston du Bousquet of the Nord railway was responsible for the development of one of the classic compound-expansion systems for steam locomotives: indeed, most of the 20th-century express passenger locomotives were of the de Glehn compound type.

De Glehn and Bousquet initially collaborated on a number of highly successful compound 4-4-0 locomotives introduced in the 1890s, but their best claim to fame was the 'Atlantic'-type 4-4-2 class first revealed in 1900 as the initial unit of 32 such locomotives for the Nord railway. The locomotives had highly pleasing lines, although some considered it odd that there were outside bearings on the two axles of the leading truck and inside bearings on the single trailing axle. The inside low-pressure cylinders were located in line with the forward axle of the leading truck and powered the leading coupled axle, while the outside high-pressure cylinders were installed in the standard position above the rear axle of the leading truck and powered the rear pair of coupled wheels.

The de Glehn Atlantic-type locomotives were used for services such as the boat trains between Paris and Calais on some of the hardest schedules in the world, but the long-term performance of the locomotives was remarkable. The type offered very low specific fuel consumption.

This gave useful operating economics, but it was also important as the power of steam locomotives was becoming limited by the ability of the fireman to shovel coal onto the grate and a relatively miserly rate of fuel consumption was a considerable bonus in this respect.

The success of the de Glehn Atlantic type was such that orders were placed for an additional 152 locomotives, including 59 for four other French operators, 79 for the Royal Prussian Union railway in Germany, and the other 14 for single operators in Egypt (10), the U.K. (3) and the U.S.A. (1). Some of these later locomotives were completed to slightly different standards, notable mainly for their greater sizes, and the technical success of the de Glehn and Bousquet compound-expansion system led the French railways to keep the system for many later classes of 4-6-0, 2-8-2, 4-6-2 and 4-8-2 locomotives. The details for the de Glehn Atlantic-type 4-4-2 locomotive included two 13.5 x 25.25-in (340 x 640-mm) high-pressure cylinders and two 22 x 25.25-in (560 x 640-mm) low-pressure cylinders, driving wheels with a diameter of 6ft 8.25in (2.04m), steam pressure of 228lb/sq in (16kg/cm²), 15,432lb (7000kg) of fuel, 6,089 U.S. gal (5,070 Imp gal; 23050 litres) of water, total weight of 78,483lb (35600kg), and overall length of 59ft 10.5in (18.247m).

During 1901 there appeared the first example of possibly the single most celebrated class of express passenger locomotive ever constructed, a type that

was built right to the end of the steam locomotive era. Oddly enough, this locomotive was not planned by one of the great locomotive-designing nations, but rather the small country of New Zealand. Here A.W. Beattie, the chief engineer of the Government Railway, felt that the country's railway system needed a locomotive with a big firebox able to burn the poor lignite coal produced at Otago on South Island.

Although Baldwin, the selected American manufacturer, recommended a Camelback 4-6-0 locomotive with a substantial firebox above the rear wheels, Beattie opted instead for a 4-6-0 development with the firebox carried by a two-wheel pony truck to create a 4-6-2. The 13 engines were quickly completed and despatched across the Pacific ocean in a process that created the generic name of the 'Pacific'-type locomotive that was to be built in very large numbers in the years to come.

The Pacific-type locomotives of the 'Q' class also had the classic type of valve gear designed during 1844 by the Belgian engineer Egide Walschaert, and lacked only two features that were added in later locomotives to create the fully definitive Pacific-type steam locomotive: these features were a superheating system and inside admission piston valves in place of outside valves.

After the implementation of some minor modifications, the locomotives of the Q class gave long service, the last of the locomotives not being retired until 1957.

The details of the Q-class locomotive included a tractive effort of 19,540lb (8863kg), two 16 x 22-in (406 x 559-mm) cylinders, driving wheels with a diameter of 4ft 1in (1.245m), steam pressure of 200lb/sq in (14kg/cm²), 11,000lb (4990kg) of fuel, 2,042 U.S. gal (1,700 Imp gal; 7728 litres) of water, total weight of 165,000lb (74844kg), and overall length of 55ft 4.5in (16.872m).

In 1902 the Chesapeake & Ohio Railroad (chartered in 1785 but beginning operations only in 1836 with the inauguration of the Louisa Railroad in Virginia) took delivery of its first Pacific-type 4-6-2 steam locomotive, the initial unit of the 'F15'-class, and in the process gained the distinction of introducing the truly definitive type of steam locomotive to American passenger services. The locomotive still possessed strong affinities with the past and had no superheating system, but was marked as something notably different from earlier types by its size and power.

The first F15-class locomotive was followed by another 26 units in the period up to 1911, and the overall success of the type is attested by the fact that virtually all of the locomotives survived in useful service until the Chesapeake & Ohio Railroad switched to diesel locomotives in the 1950s. In the later stages of their career of 50 or so years, the F15-class locomotives were gradually relegated to less important services or to lines whose bridges could not support the weight of later locomotives, and a number of upgrades were effected to

OPPOSITE: *Union Pacific No. 9000 Union Pacific-type 4-12-2 three-cylinder locomotive built by the American Locomotive company in April 1926. This was the longest non-articulated locomotive ever built and had a tender capacity of 15,000 gallons (6819 litres) of water.*

ABOVE LEFT: *Santa Fe's Class 3460 locomotive No. 3461 Pacific-type 4-6-4. It was built by the Baldwin Locomotive Works in 1937 with 84-in (2134-mm) diameter driving wheels and a tender capacity of 20,000 gallons (90920 litres).*

ABOVE RIGHT: *Santa Fe's Class 3450 locomotive No. 3456 Pacific-type 4-6-4. It was built by the Baldwin Locomotive Works in 1923 with 79-in (2007-mm) diameter driving wheels.*

incorporate features such as Walschaert valve gear, superheating and mechanical stoking systems as well as improved cabs and, in some cases, new cylinders and even new frames.

The success of the Pacific type of steam locomotive in service with American railroads was reflected in the subsequent manufacture of some 7,000 units of the same basic type for a host of operators, and the spawning of a number of derived versions for service with the Chesapeake & Ohio Railroad. These derivatives included the 'F16' class of 1913 with a larger grate area and a boost in tractive effort of almost 35 per cent, the 'F17' class of the following year with still further increases in grate area and tractive effort, and then in the period after the end of World War I the 'F18' and 'F19' classes with large 12-wheel tenders carrying increased volumes of water. The details of the F15-class locomotive in its

original form included the tractive effort of 32,400lb (14697kg), two 23.5 x 28-in (597 x 711-mm) cylinders, driving wheels with a diameter of 6ft 0in (1.829m), steam pressure of 180lb/sq in (12.7kg/cm²), 30,000lb (13608kg) of fuel, 9,000 U.S. gal (7,494 Imp gal; 34069 litres) of water, total weight of 408,000lb (185069kg), and overall length of 74ft 0in (22.555m).

Responsible for the introduction to the U.K. of the large boiler with a wide firebox, the 'Large Atlantic' class of 4-4-2 steam locomotives was designed by Henry Ivatt and built to the extent of 94 units (delivered between 1902 and 1910) for the Great Northern Railway at its own facility in Doncaster, south Yorkshire. The class reigned supreme on the southern portion of the service between London and Edinburgh up to 1921, when it was supplanted by 4-6-2 locomotives. Thereafter, the type was still used for a number of celebrated but lighter

services, and finally disappeared from service only in 1950.

In common with most of the world's truly great steam locomotives, the Large Atlantic class was essentially simple in mechanical terms but wholly modern in the features that truly counted. The cylinders were outside, the valves and valve gear were inside, and while the first 81 locomotives of the class lacked a superheating system and possessed balanced slide valves, the final 10 had a superheating system and piston valves: superheating was later retrofitted to the earlier locomotives, most of which were also adapted to piston valves. The details of the Large Atlantic-class locomotive in its superheated form included a tractive effort of 17,340lb (7865kg), two 20 x 24-in (508 x 610-mm) cylinders, driving wheels with a diameter of 6ft 8in (2.032m), steam pressure of 170lb/sq in (12.0kg/cm²), 14,500lb (6577kg) of fuel, 4,203 U.S. gal (3,500 Imp

ABOVE LEFT: *Boston & Maine's Class P-1-6 Pacific (No. 3602) prepares to leave North Station, Boston. Built in 1910, she was extensively modernized.*

ABOVE RIGHT: *Missouri Pacific locomotive No. 6509 Pacific-type 4-6-2, built in 1903 by Alco for passenger services.*

FAR LEFT: *Locomotive No. 3461 of the Santa Fe Railroad. Built by the Baldwin Works in 1937, she is a 3460-class Pacific-type 4-6-4.*

LEFT: *Boston & Maine's classic P-4-a Pacific No. 3712 about to depart Boston's North Station for Portland, Maine. 24 June 1939.*

ABOVE: *Prussian S1-class locomotive.*

ABOVE RIGHT: *Engine 3460, class leader of the Pacific-type 4-6-4 built at the Baldwin Locomotive Works in 1937.*

RIGHT: *Locomotive No. 2926,* Saint Nicholas, *a member of the Saint class of locomotives built for the Great Western Railway between 1902 and 1911.*

gal; 15911 litres) of water, total weight of 252,500lb (114534kg), and overall length of 57ft 10.25in (17.634m).

By the end of the 19th century George Jackson Churchward saw that he was likely to succeed William Dean as the chief engineer of the Great Western Railway, and also that the time was more than ripe for a virtually total renewal of the Great Western's highly diverse locomotive stock to provide a combination of greater homogeneity and superior performance. As Dean's deputy at the railway's main manufacturing plant at Swindon in Wiltshire, Churchward had been able to have many of his ideas, some of them fairly outlandish, realized in concrete form, but by the turn of the century Churchward had

come to focus on more orthodox ideas for locomotives that nevertheless embodied significant improvements over their predecessors.

This fact was reflected in the appearance during 1902 of the *Dean* (later *William Dean*) 4-6-0 steam locomotive. This seemed somewhat apart from the main stream of British locomotive thinking, but this was hardly remarkable given the close working relationship of Churchward and A.W. Gibbs, a senior engineer of the Pennsylvania Railroad in the U.S.A. The new locomotive should thus be seen as a blend of American 10-wheel design thinking and British engineering practices. In overall terms, therefore, the American 10-wheel configuration was combined with cylinders and valve chests located outside the frames

for maximum accessibility, and Stephenson valve gear inside the frames to drive the inside admission valves. Other American features were the cylinders and the smokebox, but most of the rest was of orthodox British concept. With steady refinement incorporated, this combination of American and British features became standard for the 2,000 or so locomotives of the classes designed under the supervision of Churchward and his immediate successors.

Churchward's ideas were far from fixed, however, and it should be noted that it took him a considerable time to decide whether the advantage lay with the two-cylinder 'Saint' class of 4-6-0 locomotives derived from the Dean prototype or with the four-cylinder 'Star' class of 4-6-0 locomotives.

Some 77 and 60 of these two classes were built, and it was not long before his retirement in 1921 that Churchward finally preferred the latter.

The designation Saint class was in fact applied to the two-cylinder Churchward 4-6-0 locomotives only after the completion of 32 units including three prototype locomotives. The 19 locomotives of the first production batch were delivered in 1905, and some of them operated for a short time in a 4-4-2 configuration. The second batch of 10 locomotives was delivered from 1906, and the first of this batch was also the first British locomotive with a thoroughly modern superheating system of the Schmidt type, and such a system was later retrofitted to the earlier locomotives.

From 1907 there followed 20 examples

of the genuine Saint class with a number of improved features, and finally from 1911 25 examples of the derived 'Court' subclass with a superheating system installed from the beginning together with a number of further improved features including a 0.5-in (12.7-mm) increase in cylinder diameter. One of the most important keys to the success of the Churchward locomotives was the designer's super Boiler No.1, which was used not only in the 77 units of the Saint class but also in 74 'Star' 4-6-0, three 'Frenchman' 4-4-2, 330 'Hall' 4-6-0, 80 'Grange' 4-6-0, and 150 '28XX' 2-8-0 class locomotives. A primary feature of the Boiler No.1 was the system to clean and warm the water before it reached the boiler.

Over the years, all of the Saint-class locomotives but the prototype were

OPPOSITE
LEFT: *No. 4079* Pendennis Castle,
photographed in 1967.

RIGHT: *No. 5029* Nunney Castle.

THIS PAGE
RIGHT: *Great Northern Railway's
C2 4-4-2 No. 990* Henry Oakley *pilots
C1 4-4-4 No. 251* Planet Centenarian,
*celebrating 100 years of the Doncaster
locomotive works in England.*

FAR RIGHT: *A BESA-class 2-8-0 hauling
freight in India.*

upgraded to the definitive standard typical
of the last units to be completed. It is also
worth noting that another 330 locomotives
were built to a standard described as the
Hall class, which differed from the Saint
class mainly in having driving wheels with a
diameter of 6ft 0in (1.828m) for greater
tractive effort with little reduction in
maximum speed. The details of the Saint-
class locomotive in its later guise with a
superheating system included a tractive
effort of 24,395lb (11066kg), two 18.5 x 30-
in (470 x 762-mm) cylinders, driving wheels
with a diameter of 6ft 8in (2.045m), steam
pressure of 225lb/sq in (15.8kg/cm^2),
13,500lb (6124kg) of fuel, 4,203 U.S. gal
(3,500 Imp gal; 15911 litres) of water, total
weight of 251,000lb (113854kg), and
overall length of 63ft 0.25in (19.209m).

Wholly British in concept but designed
and manufactured for service hauling main
trains in India, the 'BESA' class of 4-6-0
locomotives entered service in 1905 and
later production examples of the type are
still in effective service on the Indian
railway system.

The Indian rail network at the
beginning of the 20th century represented a
combination of private enterprise under a
concessionary system that gave the
government of India some control in return
for a guaranteed return on the operators'
investments. This was a highly beneficial
system for all concerned and, after the
relative fiasco of the first stages of Indian
railway development, in which a
proliferation of gauges was permitted
through lack of adequate overall controls,

the beginning of a more organized
nationwide rail system appeared. This
process involved the establishment of a
number of standard locomotive designs
which reflected the appreciation of
British locomotive manufacturers that
greater profitability resulted from the mass-
production of a few standard types than
the 'penny packet' production of a larger
number.

As far as the Indian rail network was
concerned, therefore, there were 'Standard
Passenger' 4-4-0, 'Standard Goods' 0-6-0,
'Heavy Goods' 2-8-0 and 'Heavy
Passenger' 4-6-0 types of locomotives for
the broad-gauge part of the system, which
had a gauge of 5ft 6in (1.68m). All of
these standard designs remained in service
virtually to the present, and the BESA

class was of the Heavy Passenger-type.

The first BESA-class locomotives were
very substantially engineered, and when
introduced were larger and more powerful
than virtually any other locomotives in India
(now divided into India, Pakistan and
Bangladesh). The design was in essence a
derivative of the 4-6-0 locomotives
produced from 1903 for the South Western
Railway by the North British Locomotive
Company of Glasgow, which manufactured
the first BESA-class locomotives for the
Indian market. The size of this market
meant that such locomotives were also built
by Vulcan Foundry, Robert Stephenson &
Company, Kitson, and William Beardmore
in the United Kingdom, while numbers were
also produced in India as that country's
industrial base became capable of the task.

The first examples had no superheating system, outside cylinders, inside slide valves and Stephenson valve gear, but this initial standard was soon upgraded to an improved pattern with outside Walschaert valve gear, outside piston valves and a superheating system. The details of the BESA-class locomotive in its definitive form included a tractive effort of 22,590lb (10247kg), two 20.5 x 26-in (521 x 660-mm) cylinders, driving wheels with a diameter of 6ft 2in (1.88m), steam pressure of 180lb/sq in (12.7kg/cm²), 16,800lb (7620kg) of fuel, 4,804 U.S. gal (4,000 Imp gal; 18184 litres) of water, total weight of 273,000lb (123833kg), and overall length of 62ft 3.25in (18.980m).

At the start of the 20th century the Prussian state railway system had to decide whether or not the superheating system was an alternative to the compound-expansion system or just an add-on element. The railway had built both simple- and compound-expansion locomotives since 1884, the former being used mainly for secondary routes and services, and the latter for primary routes and express services. The railway in fact continued with the manufacture of non-superheated compound-expansion locomotives right up to 1911, but during this period also brought into service a number of simple-expansion locomotives with a superheating system, typical of the type being the 'P6' class of 2-6-0 locomotives, some 272 of which were manufactured in the period between 1903 and 1910. The two main problems with the P6 class were the small diameter of the

driving wheels (only 5ft 3in/1.60m) that were too small for the speeds envisaged, and poor weight distribution.

In 1906 a class of 4-6-0 locomotives with a driving-wheel diameter of 5ft 9in (1.750m) made its appearance with the object of allowing a speed of 68mph (110km/h). The early locomotives were unreliable, however, and their tendency to suffer mechanical failures made them very unpopular. A cure of the class's main difficulties was found in a reduction of cylinder diameter and modification of the weight distribution, but at the same time the railway authorities came to the conclusion that as the motion and valve gear were unsuitable for speeds of 62mph (100km/h) or more, these engines should be used for secondary passenger and mixed-traffic services. This revised type was the 'P8' class, which had initially been schemed for express passenger work on a limited part of the Prussian system but now became history's most widely used and popular mixed-traffic steam locomotive.

In common with most other successful steam locomotives, the P8 class was essentially simple in its basic concept and possessed a pleasing appearance with a round-topped boiler with a narrow but lengthy firebox. At later dates, at least two other boilers were installed, but these did not change the locomotive's pleasant lines. The locomotive had a Schmidt superheating system, and the combination of this and piston valves with Walschaert valve gear provided the locomotives with one of the very highest levels of efficiency

OPPOSITE

ABOVE: *BESA-design SP 138 (KS 1921) at Jam Sahib, the* Borridge Special *from Mirpur Khas to Nawabshah.*

BELOW: *Pakistan PAK 2-15a BESA 0-6-0.*

THIS PAGE

ABOVE and RIGHT: *Pakistan Railway BESA-class 4-4-0.*

achieved in a simple-expansion engine.

Almost inevitably there were a small number of teething problems with the P8-class locomotive, but once these problems had been eliminated the P8 was manufactured in very substantial numbers as its modest axle load allowed the operation of the type over most of the Prussian rail network. The P8-class locomotive was also constructed in small numbers for the railways of Baden, Mecklenburg and Oldenburg states in Germany, and also for export. Though supposedly a locomotive for secondary passenger services, the P8-class locomotive was in fact used for primary passenger services in which there was no requirement for a speed of more than 62mph (100km/h).

By the end of World War I, some 2,350 P8-class locomotives had been manufactured for the Prussian rail network, but 628 of these had then to be handed over to other countries as part of Germany's war reparation: Belgium, for instance, received some 2,000 locomotives including 168 P8s which then remained in service up to 1966, when Belgium retired its last steam locomotives. In Germany, the loss of so many P8-class locomotives as war reparation was offset in part by the construction of more locomotives of the same type, the last of which was delivered in 1928. With the creation of the German state railway organization, the P8 class became the '38' class. Most of these locomotives were later fitted with new boilers, and their appearance was changed by the addition of feed water heaters, full-depth smoke deflectors and other outside features.

In World War II the operating region of the P8-class steam locomotives soon spread to the east as the Germans seized much of Poland in September 1939 and then from June 1941 sought to extend their empire into the U.S.S.R., and also to the south as Germany took Czechoslovakia in 1939 and then captured Yugoslavia and Greece from April 1941. This wartime exigency resulted in the use of the P8-class locomotive over a considerably larger area than before, and the type was to be seen in Czechoslovakia, Greece, Poland, Romania, U.S.S.R. and Yugoslavia, where many of the locomotives remained as the Germans were driven back in the later stages of the war. In some of the countries, the surviving locomotives of the P8 class were subjected to a modification process to bring them into line with national systems, but seldom was the successful basic design changed in any significant fashion. German production of the P8 class eventually totalled 3,438 units, and about 500 more basically identical engines were constructed in other countries, including Poland, which also created 190 examples of a derived type with a larger boiler and wider firebox on the chassis of the P8 class.

Some 2,803 example of the P8 class

ABOVE LEFT: *A P8 working in Romania. German-built locomotives were exported throughout the eastern bloc.*

ABOVE: *After World War I, of the 2,350 P8-class locomotives built for the Prussian state railway system, 628 were handed to other countries as war reparation. However, more locomotives of the same class were constructed.*

OPPOSITE: *German 03-2098 4-6-2.*

survived to the end of World War II in Germany, although many of these were unserviceable to greater or lesser extents. The creation of different rail networks in the western and eastern parts of Germany, which later became West Germany and East Germany, meant that the available P8-class locomotives were, like other surviving engines, divided between the two networks. Both organizations generally replaced the full-depth smoke deflectors with a more modern type, and some of the East German locomotives were fitted with revised exhausts of the Giesl type. The P8 class did not survive very long in West German service, for the adoption of diesel locomotives was implemented with some

speed, and by 1968 there were only 73 P8-class steam locomotives, most of them working in the south of the country, where the last of them survived to 1973 as a result of the slowing of the replacement programme. This meant that the P8 class survived longer in West than East Germany, where the final units of the class were withdrawn from service in 1972.

This was not the end of the line for the P8-class locomotive, however, for several units remained in useful service into the late 1970s in Poland and Romania. The details for the P8-class locomotive included a tractive effort of 26,764lb (12140kg), two 22.6 x 24.8-in (575 x 630-mm) cylinders, driving wheels with a diameter of 5ft 8.9in

(1.75m), steam pressure of 170.6lb/sq in (12kg/cm²), 11,023lb (5000kg) of fuel, 5,460 U.S. gal (4,696 Imp gal; 21350 litres) of water, total weight of 173,060lb (78500kg), and overall length of 61ft 0in (18.592m).

Almost certainly the type that should be regarded as the finest example of the elegance associated with the 'golden age' of steam locomotion, the 'Cardean' class and related 4-6-0 type locomotives of the Caledonian Railway marked a genuine high point in the creation and operation of the steam locomotive, not only as a means of pulling trains but also as objects of beauty in themselves and therefore worthy of lavish attention in terms of their spotless appearance (paint and brightwork) and high-

quality running as a result of excellent maintenance and servicing. Evidence of this tendency is provided by the *Cardean* itself, which was the only named locomotive of its class. The engine was the responsibility of only a single driver at any one time, and was used on only one service in any single period. The driver between 1911 and 1916, for example, was David Gibson, who drove the locomotive every weekday on the *Corridor*, the service that departed from Glasgow for Euston at 2 p.m.: the *Cardean* hauled the service as far south as Carlisle, and there turned and waited to pull the reciprocal service from Euston for an evening arrival in Glasgow. The drivers of the *Cardean*, of whom the most celebrated were James Currie and Gibson in that order, certainly believed that the locomotive was their 'property', and ensured the very highest level of maintenance for an almost legendary reliability not really affected by the occasional but inevitable breakdown resulting from mechanical failure. Even then, the *Cardean* seemed to enjoy a charmed life, for on the occasion of potentially the most dangerous of these incidents there were no casualties. The incident happened in 1909, when Currie was the driver: a crank axle broke when the train was travelling at speed, allowing one of the driving wheels to fall away down an embankment, as the train became detached from the engine. It came off the rails and was halted by its automatic Westinghouse brake system, *Cardean* remaining on the rails as Currie brought it carefully to a stop.

Designed by John Farquharson McIntosh, the five Cardean-class locomotives were constructed at the Caledonian Railway's own St. Rollox

OPPOSITE: Sir William Stanier *at Crewe North, England, 8 April 1962.*

RIGHT: *A P8 in Leipzig. After World War II, when Germany was divided into East and West, the available P8s were split between the two rail networks. In West Germany, diesel locomotives soon supplanted most of them.*

facility and entered service in 1906. The design was wholly conservative, and reflected the belief of McIntosh that the improved ride and lines resulting from the installation of the cylinders and motion inside the frames offset the disadvantages of this arrangement's poorer levels of accessibility and the higher cost of crank axles. A superheating system was added to the locomotives in 1911 and 1912, and at a later time the Caledonian Railway, itself an air-brake operator, ordered the addition of a vacuum brake so that other companies' vacuum-braked trains could be hauled. Other features of the design were a steam

servo-mechanism for the reversing gear, and a large bogie tender for longer non-stop journeys.

One of the locomotives was destroyed in the worst British rail catastrophe, which took place on 22 May 1915 at Quintinshill near Carlisle, but the other four locomotives remained in service to became part of the London Midland & Scottish Railway's fleet in the consolidation of 1923. The last of the class was *Cardean* itself, which was retired in 1930. The details of the Cardean-class locomotive included a tractive effort of 22,667lb (10282kg), two 20.75 x 26-in (527 x 660-mm) cylinders, driving wheels

with a diameter of 6ft 6in (1.981m), steam pressure of 200lb/sq in (14.1kg/cm^2), 11,000lb (4990kg) of fuel, 6,005 U.S. gal (5,000 Imp gal; 22730 litres) of water, total weight of 294,000lb (133358kg), and overall length of 65ft 6in (19.964m).

By any of several different types of criteria, the '4500' class of 4-6-2 locomotives created for the Paris-Orléans railway in 1907 could well be regarded as not just one of the classic types of steam locomotive, but possibly as 'the single' most classic locomotive intended for the hauling of express trains. The 4500-class locomotive was the first Pacific-type engine to serve in

Europe (some engines of this type having been made in the U.K. earlier in the same year but intended for service in Malaya), and in its definitive period was the most powerful and also the most efficient Pacific-type locomotive of European origin. Added to this, the 4500 was also extremely attractive and, if it can be criticized at all, its only failing was a comparatively high level of mechanical complexity.

Production of the 4500-class locomotives between 1907 and 1910 totalled 100 including 30 manufactured in the United States; but there were also 90 examples of the '3500'-class locomotive

LEFT: *Krauss-Maffei-class 03 streamline 3-cylinder express locomotive, built for the Deutsche Reichsbahn in 1940.*

BELOW LEFT: *The legendary Maffei-built locomotives steamed all over Germany, finally to be overtaken by progressive electrification of routes.*

OPPOSITE: *SNCF Class 9100.*

manufactured between 1909 and 1918 to a standard that differed from that of the 4500 class only in having a driving wheel diameter reduced by 4in (100mm).

All 190 examples of these two closely-related classes were of the four-cylinder de Glehn compound-expansion type, and with an unusual grate wide at the back but tapering to a narrow front between the frames. Later units were completed with a superheating system, and such a system was then retrofitted to a number of the earlier locomotives. Another feature was the use of piston valves in the high-pressure cylinders but there were balanced slide valves in the low-pressure cylinders.

The limitations of the 4500 class began to become apparent in the period after the end of World War I, when the rebuilding of

France's infrastructure saw the replacement of the pre-war type of wooden carriage by a stronger and more durable type of steel construction. During this period, France was also beginning the electrification of its railway network, however, so there was little in the way of financial resources for the replacement of the 4500-class locomotives. However, a development engineer on the Paris-Orléans railway, André Chapelon, successfully suggested in 1926 that the locomotives should be cycled through a relatively major reconstruction programme, which in fact began only in 1929.

The rebuilding of the 4500-class locomotives resulted in the creation of one of the definitive steam locomotive classes. Power production per unit of steam was

in place of piston valves and slide valves to provide larger and more quickly operating openings to steam and exhaust; and a double chimney for more draught and reduced back-pressure.

The improved 4500-class locomotive was so successful that the Paris-Orléans railway ordered the conversion of 31 3500-class locomotives in a similar fashion. The continuing electrification of the French railway network, especially in this core region around Paris, meant that some of the original engines became redundant to the requirements of the Paris-Orléans railway, however, but these machines were snapped up by other companies. Some 20 older locomotives were reconstructed to the Chapelon pattern for the Nord and 23 for the Ouest railways, and so successful were the locomotives in these regional operators' services that Nord ordered 20 new-build engines.

In 1932 some 16 3500-class locomotives were rebuilt to a somewhat less ambitious pattern with piston heads carrying two rather than one valve to double the area of port opened in a set distance of movement. In the same year one of the remaining 4500-class locomotives without a superheating system was rebuilt into a 4-8-0 configuration to validate the notion of creating an engine with one-third more adhesive weight and therefore better suited to the gradients typical of the line to Toulouse. The change required the use of a different boiler with a narrow firebox to fit between the rear driving wheels, but in other respects the rebuilding followed the

Chapelon pattern even though the introduction of further refinement boosted the cylinder horse power to 4,000hp. The success of the prototype conversion is attested by the fact that 11 more engines were rebuilt to the same standard during 1934, and that in 1940 some 25 more 4500-class locomotives were converted to a standard that was otherwise similar except for the addition of a mechanical stoking system.

By the 1960s the last of these Pacific-type locomotives were based at Calais to haul heavy boat trains arriving from the U.K. The locomotives were very effective in this role, being capable of hauling heavy trains up relatively steep gradients; but there could be no denial of the fact that the locomotives were heavy consumers of coal and were generally costlier to operate than simpler 2-8-2 locomotives of the '141R' class that had been delivered from the U.S. after the end of World War II to boost the reconstruction of France. The details of the 4500-class locomotive, in its form with a superheating system but before rebuilding by Chapelon, included a tractive 38,580lb (17500kg), two 16.5 x 25.6-in (420 x 650-mm) high-pressure cylinders and two 25.2 x 25.6-in (640 x 650-mm) low-pressure cylinders, driving wheels with a diameter of 6ft 2.75in (1.90m), steam pressure of 232lb/sq in (16kg/cm^2), 13,228lb (6000kg) of fuel, 5,283 U.S. gal (4,399 Imp gal; 20000 litres) of water, total weight of 300,926lb (136500kg), and overall length of 68ft 2.5in (20.79m).

Dating from much the same time as the

increased by 25 per cent, while boiler improvements allowed the generation of more steam and thereby made feasible an increase in possible cylinder horse power from 2,000hp to 3,700hp, which represented an 85 per cent increase over that of the original locomotives. Chapelon produced this transformation after a close examination of the original design to locate the features he felt were limiting overall capabilities. In this process Chapelon analyzed the whole

cycle of operations between cold water and exhaust steam, and decided that the features most needed to modernize the cycle were pre-heating of the cold feed water using waste heat from the exhaust; extra heating area in the firebox through the use of 'thermic syphons' (flattened vertical ducts); a 24 per cent increase in the size of the superheater that was also more efficient but additionally complex; enlarged steam pipes for better steam flow; use of poppet valves

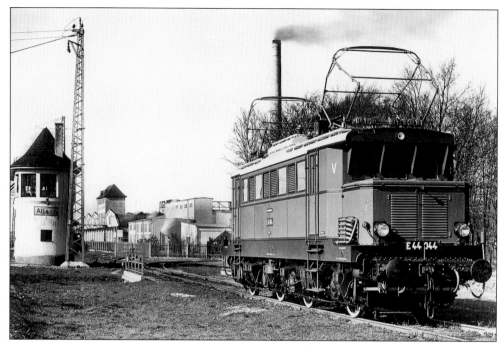

4500-class locomotives in France, the 'S3/6' class of Pacific-type 4-6-2 locomotives, introduced to the railway network of the Royal Bavarian state railway in 1909, reflected both the geographic and climatic differences of Bavaria from Prussia. The keys to this difference were the nature of Bavaria, which is considerably hillier or indeed mountainous than generally flat Prussia, and the greater flair of Heinrich Leppla, the chief designer of Maffei, the primary manufacturer of Bavarian locomotives. This flair reached it apogee in a series of Pacific-type 4-6-2 locomotives delivered for 23 years to the railways of Bavaria and Baden as well as to the German state railway that absorbed both of these operators in the 1920s.

Since 1895 the passenger locomotives

of the Bavarian railway had all been of the four-cylinder compound-expansion type, including two Atlantic-type locomotives bought during 1901 from Baldwin of the U.S.A. and, it appears, a major influence on Maffei as this company became the first European company to built locomotives of the bar frame type and also the first to cast the cylinders in substantial blocks including the smokebox saddle. All four of these cylinders powered the same axle, which in the Pacific type of locomotive was the central axle.

The first engines of this type were completed during 1908 for the railway of the state of Baden, the first locomotives for the Bavarian railway following in the next year. Production of 23 such locomotives, with a driving-wheel diameter of 6ft 1.6in

(1.87m) and a steam pressure of 212lb/sq in (15kg/cm^2), had been completed by 1911, and these were followed by 18 locomotives with a driving-wheel diameter of 6ft 6.7in (2.00m), while another 78 locomotives were manufactured between 1913 and 1924 with the original size of driving wheel. This was far from the end of the story, however, for there were a number of other batches with more limited changes such as the addition of feed-water heaters, increased axle load, and steam pressure boosted to 228lb/sq in (16kg/cm^2). The overall designation for the locomotives was S3/6 class, which detailed an express locomotive (*schnellzuglokomotiv*) with six axles of which three were powered. Germany's reparations after the end of World War I included 19 of these locomotives in the form of 16 and three for

France and Belgium respectively.

During 1925 the newly created German state railway took delivery of the first of its standard Pacific-type locomotives, but the axle load of these prevented their employment on all but the most strongly constructed lines. A class of smaller and therefore lighter Pacific types was planned for use on the rest of the German rail network, but while this was being designed and built, the national rail operator needed a Pacific-type locomotive with an axle load of no more than 18 tonnes rather than the heavier type's 20 tonnes. The obvious solution was further production of the excellent Maffei design, of which 40 were completed between 1927 and 1931. These locomotives were soon steaming all over Germany until the advent of the definitive

OPPOSITE

LEFT: King George V-class No. 6000.

RIGHT: *Krauss-Maffei-class E44 electric locomotive, built in 1936/37 for the Deutsche Reichsbahn.*

THIS PAGE
ABOVE: *Russian designers created practical locomotives for everyday service in which standardization, reliability and simplicity of operation were of critical importance.*

ABOVE RIGHT: *A Belgian 4-4-0, No. 1805, at Ostend in 1967. Belgian locomotives built in the early 20th century bore a strong conceptual resemblance to the McIntosh locomotives of the Caledonian Railway.*

'O3'-class locomotive. Even then the Maffei locomotives had a special niche, operating on the Rhine valley main line for services that included the classic *Rheingold* express before and after World War II. So successful were the locomotives in the Rhine valley that between 1953 and 1956 some 30 of the locomotives were fitted with new welded boilers. Electrification of the line finally saw the disappearance of the Maffei steam locomotives from the Rhine valley, but even so they saw a final period of useful service in Bavaria, where they handled the express services between Munich and Lake Constance, where the last of these classic locomotives was retired in 1966. The details of the S3/6-class locomotive included two 16.7 x 24-in (425 x 610-mm) high-pressure cylinders and two 25.6 x 26.4-in

(650 x 670-mm) low-pressure cylinders, driving wheels with a diameter of 6ft 1.6in (1.870m), steam pressure of 228lb/sq in (16kg/cm^2), 18,739lb (8500kg) of fuel, 7,238 U.S. gal (6,027 Imp gal; 27400 litres) of water, total weight of 328,483lb (149000kg), and overall length of 69ft 1in (21.317m).

Early in the 20th century the Belgian national railway built several classes of inside-cylinder locomotives bearing a strong conceptual relationship to the McIntosh locomotives of the Caledonian Railway. During 1904, however, there began a new era in the hands of J. B. Flamme, who was interested in the French type of compound-expansion locomotive and secured the loan of such an engine for evaluation. This French locomotive was clearly so much

better than existing Belgian engines that Flamme ordered 12 similar locomotives, and then 57 of a compound-expansion 4-6-0 design. Flamme's next step was the manufacture of four 4-6-0 locomotives to a new design, and in these he was also to undertake an investigation of the superheating system in simple- and compound-expansion locomotives. This process permitted Flamme to opt for the simplicity and lower cost of the non-compound locomotive, although he appreciated that for the largest classes there were advantages in the use of four cylinders to give the improved level of balance revealed by the four-cylinder compound-expansion locomotives.

The result was two classes of very large locomotives, namely a Pacific-type 4-6-2 for

employment on express services and a 2-10-0 type for employment on freight services. The boilers of the two classes were basically similar except for a few small differences in the size of their fireboxes, and the limiting factor for length was the upper weight figure for the 2-10-0 type. The boiler would have appeared short on any Pacific-type locomotive, but this fact was accentuated by a number of other features, and by the European concepts of the period the boiler was odd as it possessed a very large grate for the burning of low-grade coal. Walschaert valve gear was used for the valves of the two outside cylinders, and rocking shafts were employed to operate the valves of the two inside cylinders that powered the leading axle.

Between 1910 and 1928, 28 of these engines were manufactured, with 30 more following in 1929 and 1930 with a grate of smaller size and shortened rear end, changes that knocked 5 tonnes off the weight. Known as the '10' class under a later classification, these locomotives worked the express routes connecting Brussels with Liège and Luxembourg, and were highly effective.

The Belgian national railway started a major refurbishment of its stock after World War I, and within the context of this programme fitted larger superheating systems, double chimneys for improved draught, strengthened the frames at the

front, and there were a number of detail enhancements. The programme continued with the addition of smoke deflectors and feed-water heaters, and bogie tenders from German war-reparation engines replaced the original six-wheeled tenders. Spurred by the success of Chapelon's efforts in France, the Belgians launched another improvement effort in 1938 with features such as enlarged steam pipes, greater superheating area, and the replacement of the Legein double-chimney exhaust by the Kylchap pattern. These changes did little for the appearance of the locomotives, but did produce the increase in performance and tractive effort that had been demanded. It was 1959 before the last of these locomotives, in fact one of the first-series machines, was finally retired. The details of the 10 class included a tractive effort of 43,651lb (19800kg), four 19.7 x 26-in (500 x 660-mm) cylinders, driving wheels with a diameter of 6ft 6in (1.98m), steam pressure of 199lb/sq in (14kg/cm^2), 15,432lb (7000kg) of fuel, 6,340 U.S. gal (5,279 Imp gal; 24000 litres) of water, total weight of 352,734lb (160000kg), and overall length of 70ft 3in (21.404m).

With the retirement of Francis Webb as its chief locomotive engineer during 1903, the London & North Western Railway was able to start the process of replacing the compound-expansion and other obsolescent locomotives whose retention the autocratic

OPPOSITE

ABOVE: *Chelyabinsk railway station in what is now the Russian Federation.*

BELOW: *About 2,400 Russian Su-class locomotives were built over 15 years and they became the definitive standard Russian locomotives to haul passenger trains.*

THIS PAGE

ABOVE: *The* Caledonian, *resplendent in the livery of the London, Midland & Scottish Railway (LMS), leaves Crewe for Carlisle.*

RIGHT: *LMS Duchess-class 4-6-2 locomotive at Bury, England. This class of locomotive was the most powerful ever to run in that country.*

Webb had demanded. Under the supervision of George Whale and W. T. Bowen-Cooke, Webb's immediate successors, over a period of 10 years the company acquired 336 4-4-0 and 4-6-0 express locomotives, engines manufactured at the company's Crewe plant, which undertook the whole process between the receipt of raw materials and the delivery of complete locomotives, a process for which Webb must take a good deal of the credit.

Four types of express locomotive were constructed at Crewe in this period, and while three of them were useful if not wholly inspired types, the fourth was truly outstanding. This was the later of the two 4-4-0 types, the great 'George V' class of locomotives of which the first was delivered during 1910. The design was in essence a much improved development of the 'Precursor' class of 1903 with more modern features such as piston valves and a superheating system. Some 90 George V-class locomotives were built, to which must be added a further 64 conversions from the Precursor class as well as another 10 from the 'Queen Mary' class of 4-4-0 locomotives without a superheating system.

Despite their limited 4-4-0

configuration, these locomotives hauled much of the prestige passenger traffic between Euston and stations to the north. In the George V class everything was consciously made as simple as possible. The outer firebox wrapper was of the round top rather than the more complicated Belpaire type, and while the cylinders were of the inside type, the use of the Joy-type valve gear, with rods and slides in the same vertical plane as the connecting rods, created a situation in which all the inside motion was readily reached for lubrication and maintenance. The Joy-type valve gear was

not quite as efficient as it could have been, possibly because it had been 'improved' for this application and thereby made more complex, while the Schmidt piston valves were also prone to wear: both these features led to high coal and steam consumption, but careful maintenance alleviated the problem.

During 1923 the virtual multitude of British railway companies was consolidated into four large organizations, the George V-class locomotives thereby coming into the ownership of the London Midland & Scottish Railway, a company controlled largely by ex-Midland Railway men who had a low regard for all locomotives originating outside this company. It was hardly surprising, therefore, that the retirement of these effective locomotives started as early as 1935, ending with the retirement of the last unit in 1948. The details of the George V-class locomotive included a tractive effort of 20,066lb (9102kg), two 20.5 x 26-in (521 x 660-mm)

cylinders, driving wheels with a diameter of 6ft 9in (2.057m), steam pressure of 175lb/sq in (12.3kg/cm^2), 13,440lb (6096kg) of fuel, 3,603 U.S. gal (3,000 Imp gal; 13638 litres) of water, total weight of 212,800lb (96526kg), and overall length of 57ft 2.75in (17.445m).

The 'S' class of massive 2-6-2 steam locomotives introduced in 1911 for the Russian Ministry of Ways of Communication may have been the most prolific of all steam locomotives as its manufacture lasted for 40 years and its usage for more than 60 years. Despite the fact that steam-locomotive design in Russia was generally entrusted to academics, who often exploited the chance to create extraordinary prototype machines more notable for their theory than their practice, but were nonetheless able to create truly practical locomotives for everyday service, in which simplicity of concept and operation was all important for reliable use in Russia's vast and diverse geography.

Despite the many aspersions cast on it by large numbers of the ill-informed, both at the time and later, the tsarist government of pre-revolutionary Russia was in fact far ahead of its time in matters of standardization, and this process continued after the Soviet Revolution of 1917 and the tumult of the years that followed.

The S class of 2-6-2 locomotives was a standard design for general use among Russia's many independent railways. The 'S' stood for the Soromovo works at Nizhnii Novgorod (later Gorkiy) where the class was built, and about 900 such excellent

locomotives were manufactured before the revolution. The design was an early example of what was in effect the standard definitive form of steam locomotive with two cylinders, Walschaert valve gear, a wide firebox, a superheating system, and compensated springing.

The 'Su' class of larger, improved locomotives was first manufactured during 1926 at the Kolomna plant near Moscow in 1926. This subclass, of which about 2,400 were completed over a 15-year period, may be regarded as the definitive standard, and the 'u' in the designation stood for *usilennyi* (strengthened). The wheel base, boiler and cylinders were all enlarged but there was no increase in the boiler pressure over the modest figure inherited from the baseline S class, reflecting the fact that the cost-conscious Soviets, with a non-competitive system, felt that a higher boiler pressure would add unnecessary production and maintenance costs.

After the end of World War II in 1945, manufacture was resumed at the Soromovo plant and continued until 1951, by which time some 3,750 S-class locomotives had been built. Variants comprised some 'Sv'-class locomotives built in 1915 for the standard-gauge line from Warsaw south toward Vienna, and some 'Sum'-class units with a system for pre-heating the combustion air. Many of the S-class locomotives burned not coal but oil, a fuel that had been introduced into Russia as early as 1880 and soon became relatively common. The details of the S-class locomotive included a tractive effort of

30,092lb (13650kg), two 22.5 x 27.5-in (575 x 700-mm) cylinders, driving wheels with a diameter of 6ft 0.75in (1.85m), steam pressure of 185lb/sq in (13kg/cm^2), 39,683lb (18000kg) of fuel, 6,010 U.S. gal (5,004 Imp gal; 22750 litres) of water, total weight of 370,370lb (168000kg), and overall length of 77ft 10.5in (23.738m).

OPPOSITE
ABOVE: *Krauss-Maffei Class 50 heavy locomotive, built in 1939 for the Deutsche Reichsbahn (German Railway). This engine was withdrawn in 1965.*

BELOW: *Maffei-Zoelly Class T18 turbine locomotive, built for the Deutsche Bundesbahn between 1925 and 1928.*

THIS PAGE
ABOVE: *A Class A4 streamline 4-6-2, the famous A4 Pacific, which still holds the world's speed record for a steam locomotive. It is probably the favourite locomotive of British rail enthusiasts.*

BELOW: *A unique line-up of A4s at the National Railway Museum, York, England. Nearest the camera is the* Mallard.

Picture Acknowledgements

Ann Ronan Picture Library,
London: Title page, pages 6, 10
above right, 12 above, 19 below
right
*Association of American
Railroads: page 16 all
*Baltimore & Ohio Railroad
Museum: page 23 below
*Burlington Northern Railroad:
page 31 above left
*Canadian National Railway: page
19 above right
*Chicago, Burlington & Quincy
Railroad: page 26
*C&O Historical Society: page 40
above right
Colin Garratt: pages 50 below, 51
both, 52 right, 53, 55
*Deutsche Bundesbahn: page 56
below
*Deutsches Museum, Munich:
pages 20 above right and below
(both), 21 all
*Great Northern Railway: pages
29 below left, 36
Image Select: page 37
*Italian State Railways: page 37
below
J.M. Jarvis: page 42 above and
below left
*Krauss-Maffei AG: pages 56
above, 58 right, 62 both
Milepost: pages 24, 60 below
Military Archives & Research
Services, Lincolnshire, England:
pages 7 below, bottom left and
bottom right, 8–9 all, 10 above left,
13 above, below 1st, 3rd and 4th
from the left, 14 all, 15, 17 both, 18
both, 22, 28 both, 29 below right, 31
below right, 35 above left, 39 above
right, 40 top left, 41 top, 46 above
left, 46 below right, 47 top left
*Missouri Pacific Railroad: page
46 above right
*New Zealand Railway and
Locomotive Society: pages 38–39
below, 39 above left, 40 below, 41
below
*Novosti: pages 59 left, 60 above
*Northern Pacific Railroad: pages
23 above right, 27 below
©Railfotos, Millbrook House
Limited, Oldbury, W. Midlands,
England: pages 2, 4–5, 11, 12
below, 13 below (2nd from left), 19
below right, 29 above, 30, 31 above
right, below left, 32 all, 33 above,
34 both, 35 above right and below,
37 above, 38 above, 39 below right,
42 below right, 43, 47 below, 48
both, 49 both, 50 above, 52 left, 54,
58 left, 59 right, 61 both, 63 both
*Santa Fe Railroad: pages 33
below, 45 both, 46 below left, 47 top
right
*SNCF: page 57
*Southern Pacific Railroad: pages
20 above left, 23 above left
*Union Pacific Railroad Museum:
pages 7 below, 27 top, 44

* Print/transparency through
Military Archives & Research
Services, Lincolnshire, England.